AMERICAN

POLITICAL

BOSSES

AND

MACHINES

American Political Bosses and Machines

FRED J. COOK

FRANKLIN WATTS | NEW YORK | LONDON

ILLUSTRATION CREDITS

Library of Congress: pp. 37, 138, 141.
Ohio Historical Society Library: pp. 134–5, 136, 137.
California Historical Society, San Francisco: pp. 139, 140.
United Press International: p. 142.

Library of Congress Cataloging in Publication Data

Cook, Fred J
  American political bosses & machines.

  1. Corruption (in politics)—United States—History.
2. Municipal government—United States—History.
I. Title.
JS401.C66   320.9'73'09   73-6777
ISBN 0-531-02646-9

Contents

1

---◆◆◆---

The Political
Boss

LINCOLN STEFFENS WAS probably the greatest authority America has
produced on the nature of that uniquely American animal—the
political boss.

Steffens was the leader of a band of crusading journalists who, in
the early 1900s, earned for themselves the nickname of "muckrakers"
because they dug up and exposed the hidden dirt underlying the
placid face of American society. Steffens was a small, slim man with a
bushy mustache and a sharp-pointed little goatee. Well-educated, mild-
mannered, he liked to meet and question the political bosses whom he
was exposing. He was the kind of interviewer who led them on in a
gentle, quizzical manner; but the nature of his penetrating questions
seemed to require unavoidable, surprising, and, indeed, highly disturbing answers.

Such was the alert, disturbing newspaperman who went into
Philadelphia in early 1903 to write another story on municipal corruption. Steffens was almost certain of what he would find there. He
had studied intimately the power and corruption of New York's Tammany Hall, the most notorious political machine in the nation. Ear-
lier he had probed the power of political bosses in St. Louis, Pittsburgh,
and other cities; and he had become convinced that the political-boss
system—and its attendant corruption—was a fixture of American life
and operated in similar fashion everywhere. Nevertheless, when he

began to poke into the situation in Philadelphia, this experienced and case-hardened reporter was in for a shock.

It began with a talk with his hotel manager. The man told Steffens that, when he had gone to vote in the last election, he was told that he could not cast his ballot because he had voted already. It developed that machine underlings had already cast votes in both his and his brother's names. After a furious argument, the hotelman was allowed to vote, but then, he said, "they called in a couple of gangsters to offset my ballot by voting the other way—in the names of George Washington and Benjamin Franklin."

As Steffens knew, there was nothing unusual about political machines using squads of repeaters to cast fraudulent votes, sometimes under names garnered from tombstones in the cemeteries. But the Philadelphia organization, in its impudence, had added a special fillip to the fraud: it had its repeaters use "all the names of the signers of the sacred Constitution of the United States" and names culled from the "membership lists of the swell clubs."

What was being done about all this? Nothing. Steffens found that a spirit of absolute hopelessness pervaded Philadelphia. "There is nothing to be done," his hotelman said. "We have tried reforms over and over again; we have striven to beat this game; and we never got anywhere."

One incident above all others showed just how brash the gang could be. A courageous newspaper, the *North American,* owned by the son of John Wanamaker, the merchant prince, kept hammering away at the political machine. The editor, threatened with assassination, simply moved his desk away from a window and kept right on publishing the damning facts. The contest eventually built up to a showdown. The newspaper discovered that Mayor Ashbridge intended to give away, absolutely free, a very valuable street railway franchise. John Wanamaker offered to pay the city $2.5 million for the same franchise. Not to be intimidated, the mayor went right ahead with the original plan—and signed away the multi-million-dollar rights for nothing.

How could such things happen? How was it possible? To get the answers, Steffens went to see Israel W. (Iz) Durham, the Philadelphia boss. He found a slight man, with wise quick eyes, sitting relaxed behind a large desk. One look told Steffens that Durham was not a well man. They began to talk, and the boss and the reporter made a deal:

Durham would answer Steffens' questions first: then he wanted Steffens to answer some of his own.

Steffens went at once to the heart of the puzzle that baffled him. The Ashbridge administration had burst forth with what he called "a volcanic eruption" of franchise steals. There had been no attempt at concealment; it had been a wide-open flood of corruption that had poured forth like some swollen river bursting through a dam. As Steffens told Durham, "You could put over one of those steals in New York or anywhere else, but one would be enough to strain any machine I know of. But five—or more!"

The boss just smiled. That was the whole point, he said; he and his cronies had decided that "it was exactly the five—or more—that would save us."

Steffens was bewildered by this reasoning, so Iz Durham explained:

"If we did any one of these things alone, the papers and the public would concentrate on it, get the facts, and fight. But we reasoned that if we poured them all out fast and furious, one, two, three—one after the other—the papers couldn't handle them all and the public would be stunned and—give up. Too much."

This, then, was the explanation for the mood of hopelessness that Steffens had found in Philadelphia, and he concluded that the Durham machine was even more sophisticated than Tammany Hall in New York. Iz Durham agreed and put his philosophy in a few, blunt words: "We know that public despair is possible and that that is good politics."

The boss explained that the machine had accepted a new "reform" city charter that represented the last desperate throw of the dice by idealists in their effort to clean up the city and rid it of political corruption. The machine had swallowed the charter whole, the way a boa constrictor ingests a live victim—and then had gone right on with politics as usual, its corruption no whit diminished. This, too, had contributed to the city-wide despair of Philadelphia.

Lights began to flash in Steffens' mind, and he began to tell Iz Durham what he saw.

"Political corruption is, then, a process," he said. "It is not a temporary evil, not an accidental wickedness, not a passing symptom of the youth of a people. It is a natural process by which a democracy is gradually made over into a plutocracy. . . . If this process goes on, then this American republic of ours will be a government that represents the organized evils of a privileged class."

As Steffens talked, Iz Durham began to be disturbed. He had, as Steffens later wrote, the sharpest mind to be found in Philadelphia, and he saw all the implications in Steffens' reasoning. Yet Durham had difficulty in understanding what he had done "that's so rotten wrong." He had grown up in the system; he had taken the system as he had found it and had used it as others had used it before him. He had been loyal to his friends and supporters, to his ward, and to his party; by his own lights, he had been honorable—and yet Steffens' analysis pictured him as an agent of evil. What had he done that was "so rotten wrong"?

Durham didn't want his answer right away, he wasn't ready for it yet; but he and Steffens agreed that later, when he was ready, he would summon Steffens and Steffens would come. The summons came when Durham was on his death bed, and Steffens returned to Philadelphia to see the boss and answer his question.

The answer was one that struck at the very heart of Durham's faith in himself, at the one virtue above all others that the boss had believed he possessed—his loyalty to friends and party. For Steffens told him that his major sin had been *disloyalty*. Steffens later wrote that "my answer, as it gradually convinced him, was devastating. He was a born leader of the common people, I reasoned; he had taught them to like and trust him, even with their votes; he had gathered up and organized the power which lay in their ballots, their trust and their loyalty to him; and he, the good fellow, had taken his neighbors' faith and sovereignty and turned it into franchises and other grants of the common wealth, which he and his gang had sold to rich businessmen and other enemies of the people. He was a traitor to his own."

Iz Durham understood. He did not evade; he did not deny. After what Steffens called "a long, wan silence," he said: "Say, I sure ought to go to hell for that. . . ." Steffens then turned around and did his best to reassure him, reminding him that his God was merciful and forgiving.

This dialogue between Steffens and Durham, the muckraking reporter and the political boss, throws its own harsh and revealing light on a system that had operated in America for nearly seventy years before their time and that has continued, with few changes, for some seventy years since. The political boss has played a key role in American history and has wielded a power disproportionate to whatever public position he may hold. It is important, then, to understand how he came into being, how his power has grown and flourished, what effect he has had on all our lives.

D. W. Brogan in his *Politics in America* argues that the political machine is a distinctly American institution because in the United States more than in other nations a great part of the political power resides in non-official hands. He finds that the political-boss system, with all its attendant evils, grew because American society developed in such rapid, unstable fashion, with towns mushrooming into cities almost overnight, hundreds of thousands of immigrants crowding into residential areas suddenly turned into slums, a restless, shifting, ever moving population. Hence, wrote Brogan, the political machine performed a function: "It gave a kind of coherence to a society in perpetual flux, in which even the natives were bewildered by the new problems of urban life in cities growing like the prophet's gourd. And it did this at a price. To the poor it gave favors; if it controlled the police, it could moderate its zeal; it could give and withhold minor favors like peddlers' licenses; it could arrange for naturalization; it could act as a kind of charity operating society, helping with coal and food in domestic crises; and, with its parades and excursions, it provided circuses as well as bread."

The help that the boss gave to the poor, to the followers in his own ward, was always simple and direct and obvious. The family that got food or coal in the heart of a bitter winter knew their benefactor and were grateful. This gratitude meant votes. The deals that were made on the higher, more remote levels of city government were often tangled in the intricacies of high finance. They did not impinge as did the boss's good deeds directly on the lives of the people. As Brogan concludes: "What it [the machine] did for the poor may have been far less than what it did against them, but what it did for them was very visible; what it did against them was usually, though not always, invisible."

Such, then, was the basis of the American political-boss system. Operating on two levels separated from each other by a gulf of interests and understanding, nourished by a legend, it first developed in full-fledged form in New York in the political machine that was to become a national symbol—Tammany Hall.

2

---·◆·---

Tammany Hall

LONG BEFORE THE white man began to explore the wild, vast American continent, there was, so legend has it, a great Indian chief who lived somewhere west of the Allegheny Mountains. He was a famous hunter, warrior, and statesman. He was known as Chief Tammany.

According to Indian lore, Chief Tammany was the savior of his people because he defeated the Evil Spirit in a series of great personal duels. When the Evil Spirit made common plants spew out poisons, Chief Tammany countered by setting fire to all the prairies, creating such a blaze that he even singed the hide of the fleeing Evil One.

Furious at this first defeat, the Evil Spirit concocted an even more devilish plan. He sent a whole army of rattlesnakes against Tammany. But the great chief turned back this invasion by jumping on the heads of the rattlesnakes and killing them.

The second defeat made the Evil Spirit even more desperate for revenge, and he marshalled a horde of mammoths and sent them to attack Tammany. Again, the wily chief proved too much for his foe. He dug deep pits, with sharp spears concealed in them; then he placed salt licks behind the traps he had fashioned. When the mammoths charged toward the salt licks, they tumbled into the hidden pits and were impaled on the spears.

Foiled for the third time, the Evil Spirit went literally berserk. He ripped apart the skies with thunderbolts, and a deluge such as had not been seen since the days of Noah descended upon the land. The Evil One then constructed a dam across a lake near Detroit. The torrential rains backed up water behind the dam, causing all the Great Lakes to overflow in a flood that threatened to drown Chief Tammany and his whole tribe. But again the Indian chieftain proved more than a match for the evil spirit. He scooped out a ditch, now the channel of the Ohio River, and the flood waters poured harmlessly away; the rain eventually ended—and the Great Lakes fell back to their normal levels. All that was left to remind future generations of this final, titanic duel was the rapids of Detroit and Niagara Falls.

Such was the ancient Indian legend that was picked up and became popular throughout colonial America in the days before the Revolution, giving the name of Tammany to any number of widely scattered societies, only one of which has endured—New York's Tammany Hall.

Just why the legend of Chief Tammany should have been so widely popular in early America is hard to say. But the fact remains that it was. In 1732 the Schuylkill Fishing Company, a Philadelphia social club, adopted Tammany as its patron saint. Similar clubs soon sprang up, and it became traditional to hold festivals on May 1, which was known as "Saint Tammany Day."

As opposition to British rule mounted in the days before the Revolution, Tammany clubs multiplied throughout the seaboard colonies, where they became increasingly active in the patriot cause. During the Revolution, indeed, "Saint Tammany" became the patron saint of the Continental Army. With the end of the war in 1783, and independence achieved, most of these politicized Tammany clubs simply died away. Only in New York was the legend of Tammany revived in a new and more powerful form.

Two weeks after the inauguration of George Washington as the first President of the United States in 1789, New Yorkers formed a society called the Tammany Society or, sometimes, the Columbian Order. Its members were sworn to uphold the Constitution and preserve liberty. It was not at first a political club. Only the "best" people of the time belonged, and Tammany became prominent in the social life of the city. Its colorful spectacles always attracted large audiences. Almost half a century was to pass before Tammany became the powerful political structure that has been known ever since as Tammany Hall.

The change in Tammany went hand-in-hand with changes in the nation. It is perhaps hard today to realize what a small, rural nation the United States originally was. When George Washington was President, there was not a single city as we know cities today. The census of 1790 showed only five towns with a population of more than 8,000 persons.

In this kind of society, the most prominent men in local areas naturally became the leaders of the people and the directors of public affairs. There were, in the beginning, no political parties as we now know them. Leadership was invested in the relative few who, by virtue of their wealth or birth or outstanding abilities, became recognized as the spokesmen for their sections. In New York, for decades, this kind of leadership was exercised by the Knickerbocker aristocracy, who were descended from the old Dutch burghers of the original New Amsterdam, and who had a love of order and moderation.

It was not until after 1825 that New York began to change—and change radically. The opening of the Erie Canal brought the produce of the developing West to the Hudson River and down that river to New York, which rapidly became a great port and the hub of industry and commerce.

In the short span of twenty years, the entire complexion of the city changed. With booming business came a flood of immigrants—the poor and hopeless of Europe, speaking a variety of tongues; shrewd New Englanders and sharp-eyed upstaters, fiery Southerners, adventurers of every kind, all drawn to this new magnet of trade, all determined to make their fortunes as quickly as possible—and not caring how they did it. New York changed from the placid Dutch village in which chains were stretched across the street on Sundays, so that no vehicles could rattle over the cobblestones to disturb the Sabbath quiet, into a wide-open, brawling, frontier-type boom town, with all the vices of such places. Where, in 1820, the city had barely 100,000 residents, some twenty years later it had half a million.

The urban sprawl with which we are today so familiar had begun. The old families, whose fine residences had graced the lower part of Manhattan Island, were crowded out and displaced by the horde of immigrants. Noisome, incredible slums—worse even than those we know today—swiftly developed. City services were virtually non-existent.

Until 1844 the city had no police force, no fire department. A few watchmen wearing leather caps came on duty at dusk and patrolled the streets until dawn. When fires broke out, volunteer firemen, hauling their equipment behind them, tried in their fumbling fashion to put out the flames. Water supplies were often inadequate for the task, and on several occasions whole sections of the jerry-built city were destroyed. There was no health department, no sewage system. Garbage collected in the gutters, and hogs roamed the streets at will.

Charles Dickens, the famous British novelist, was so shocked by the crudeness of American society that he wrote this description:

"Once more on Broadway! Here are the same ladies in bright colors, walking to and fro. We are going to cross here. Take care of the pigs. Two portly sows are trotting behind this carriage, and a select party of half-a-dozen gentlemen hogs have just now turned the corner . . . They are the city scavengers, these pigs. Ugly brutes they are, having, for the most part, scanty brown backs, like the lids of old horse-hair trunks. At this hour, just as evening is closing in, you will see them roaming towards bed by scores, eating their way to the last."

The immigrants and the impoverished lived in the most horrible conditions, whole families crowded into dank cellars or into firetrap tenements containing interior rooms without windows, deprived of light and air. In these miserable surroundings, crime flourished. Gangs of ruffians often beat and robbed respectable citizens on the streets in broad daylight. At night, no one in his right senses ventured forth.

What had been a stable sober city, its mood determined by its Dutch heritage, had become in an incredibly short span of years a chaotic melting pot over which the old-line leadership could no longer exert influence. This vacuum and this chaos led to the creation of a new power structure in American life—the political machine, dominated by an all-powerful political boss.

Such were the forces that transformed Tammany Hall from a social club of the highly respectable into a powerful political organization. And such was the atmosphere that produced the first great political boss, a man who ever since has remained in popular imagination a symbol of his kind—William Marcy "Boss" Tweed.

3

---◆---

Boss Tweed and
the Tweed Ring

THE MAN WHO was to become the first all-powerful boss of New York—and who was to set a record for public thievery that has never been surpassed—was born in New York on April 3, 1823, in a small house in what was known as the Cherry Hill section, about half-way between the East River and the City Hall he was later to dominate.

William Marcy Tweed's ancestors were Scottish, and the first of the American line had landed in New York with his bride in the 1750s. Tweed's father, Richard, was a hard-working furniture-maker, specializing in Windsor chairs. The future political boss was the last of Richard Tweed's five children, and he was by all odds the most intelligent and most powerfully built.

In his prime, William Tweed stood well over six feet tall and weighed 270 pounds, all of it bone and muscle. He was a handsome man with a dark brown beard,."fine dark brown hair and clear gritty eyes." His physical prowess had marked him as a leader from boyhood. When older boys taunted him, he hammered them into subjection with his fists, and before long he was roaming the streets at the head of his own Cherry Hill youth gang.

The New York in which young Tweed grew to manhood was a city in the throes of radical change. Tweed's birth coincided almost exactly with the beginning of the era of tumultuous upheaval that was to make New York a brawling boom town; and his youth was spent, his convictions formed, in a brutalized city—one without morals or conscience in which, it seemed, every man had his price.

Brothels operated openly on Broadway. Newspapers denounced vice and sin on the one hand, and on the other accepted the advertisements of gamblers, prostitutes, and abortionists. One of the most powerful personages in the city was a woman abortionist known as Madame Restell. She began plying her trade about 1835, and in the succeeding decades she amassed an incredible fortune, running into millions of dollars at a time when a million was worth many times what it is today. She advertised openly in the newspapers. She dominated the police and the courts. She even outbid the Catholic Archbishop of New York for a plot of land at Fifth Avenue and 52nd Street; and there she built one of the showiest mansions in the city on the very site the archbishop had wanted for his cathedral. In her adjoining stables, even the stalls for her horses were made of mahogany.

Madame Restell was only one of the uglier symptoms of an ugly time. It was the fashion in the better homes to hire little girls of five or six years of age to do the housework; only the more humane specified in their advertisements that a girl whom they wanted for such work must be at least ten years old. At almost any time during these mid-century years from 1830 to 1860, hordes of homeless children, both boys and girls, roamed the streets like small, wild animals. They numbered anywhere from 10,000 to 30,000 at any given time, scrounging a living however they could. Little girls sometimes swept the sidewalks, helping to clean the filthy streets, their only reward a few pennies that some kind passersby might drop into their hands. These children were the human refuse from the unspeakable tenements. And it was from their ranks that the army of thieves, thugs, and prostitutes was recruited.

In a city that seemed to have lost all sense of decency, politics became increasingly depraved. The election of 1841, when Tweed was eighteen, marked a turning point. Gangsters were openly recruited by both Whigs and Democrats, and brass knuckles and other forms of brutality were used by both sides in the attempt to keep opposition voters from the polls. In succeeding elections, the skullduggery became even worse. Convicts were let out of prison, housed in city hotels, and often allowed to escape after they had obligingly cast their votes for the party in power. Where in the past ward politics had been in control of the shopkeepers and businessmen, political power now came to be exercised increasingly by thugs. The respectables were mere window-dressing for swaggering bullies like Isaiah Rynders, who headed an organization known as the Empire Club. Rynders was a crook and gambler; his head and body, badly scarred by the slashes of bowie knives, bore mute testimony to his brawling life as a professional bruiser. Yet it was he and such as he, commanding their legions of knuckle dusters and dirk men, who became increasingly powerful in determining the results on election day.

William Marcy Tweed, who, as his father's favorite, had received a better than average education for those days, observed all of this with his sharp mind and drew from it, it would appear, his own inevitable conclusions. At the end of his career, after his downfall, he declared in a statement to an official stenographer:

"The fact is New York politics were always dishonest—long before my time. There never was a time when you couldn't buy the Board of Aldermen [the municipal governing body]. A politician in coming forward takes things as they are. This population is too hopelessly split up into races and factions to govern it under universal suffrage, except by the bribery of patronage, or corruption."

Even before he became involved in politics himself, Tweed observed at first hand the corruptive tactics of the contending parties. The year was 1844 when Tweed was just twenty-one and able to cast his first vote in a Presidential election. James K. Polk was the Democratic candidate. He was opposed on the Whig line by Henry Clay, the great senator from Kentucky and the author of compromises that for a time postponed the Civil War. Tweed had an excellent head for figures and a lively curiosity; he always wanted to know just what made things work. And so, after casting his ballot, he spent some time around the polling places to see what he could see.

He soon discovered that there was a lot to see. Watchers at the polls took up positions at the curbs outside and openly bargained for votes. Tweed saw votes bought and paid for within a few feet of the polls. He saw thugs, who were well paid for their services, voting time and time again—though not, as later in Philadelphia, in the names of George Washington and Benjamin Franklin. Tweed asked for the registration figures. He was told only 45,000 persons were eligible to vote —and, of course, not all of the eligibles ever voted. Even in a Presidential election in which interest was high, there would be at least 8 per cent who wouldn't vote. Tweed, who kept the books in the brush factory of his father-in-law, Joseph C. Skaden, easily figured out that not more than 41,400 votes could possibly be cast for Polk and Clay. Great was his astonishment, therefore, when he learned the next day that the two Presidential candidates between them had polled 55,000 votes—10,000 more than the total of qualified voters in the city! No stuffing of the ballot box could have been more brazen.

It was soon after this that Tweed himself began to travel the political road. His route into politics lay through the volunteer fire companies. As a boy, like many boys, he had been entranced by the gleaming fire engines and the heroic aura that surrounded firemen dashing out on their rescue missions. And so, in 1848, when a new fire company was formed in his neighborhood, he promptly joined it. His physical prowess and force of character soon made him a leader. The company adopted the name he suggested: Americus Engine Company Number 6, soon to be popularly known as the Big Six. In July, 1849, Tweed was elected assistant foreman, and just a year later he became foreman, the boss of Big Six.

This prominence in one of the city's elite volunteer fire companies led directly to Tweed's first plunge into politics. In the same year in which he became foreman (1850), he sought election as Assistant Alderman from the Seventh Ward. The volunteer firemen were a close-knit fraternity and formed a solid voting bloc, giving Tweed a basis of strength. He was also known as a prosperous young businessman whose family had lived in the ward for three generations. And so, though the Democratic Party was badly divided in that year, as it so often is, Tweed ran a strong race, losing to his Whig rival by the narrow margin of only 47 votes.

His defeat pleased his family, whose members regarded politics as a dirty business in which he should not meddle; but Tweed himself, accustomed now to the satisfactions that come from success and leadership, was mortified. His pride made it inevitable that he should try again, and so he did the very next year, 1851, when he was nominated for Alderman. The Democratic Party was badly split over the increasingly crucial slavery issue, and Tweed knew that he faced the strong probability of a second defeat. And so he adopted a tactic that many a political boss has used ever since: he put a straw man into the race to split the Whig opposition. He persuaded a friendly and well-liked Whig to run as an independent—a strategy that drained off 206 votes, just enough to enable Tweed to defeat his Whig opponent by the narrow margin of 1,384 votes to 1,336.

As an Alderman, Tweed now sat on the Common Council of New York. This consisted of a band of rogues who were to go down in history as The Forty Thieves; and Tweed had hardly warmed his seat before he became a leader in the larceny.

The council was composed of the city's twenty Aldermen and twenty Assistant Aldermen. These Aldermen had king-like powers in their districts. They appointed all policemen of whatever rank; they and they alone granted saloon licenses; and as a body, acting for the city as a whole, they awarded franchises to operate bus and streetcar lines and ferries. The Aldermen had other vital powers. Each sat as a Justice in the Mayor's Court (no longer in existence) and as a judge in the criminal courts. The Alderman might have no knowledge whatever of the law, but he had the power to pick grand juries, to rule on fine legal issues, and to decide, in effect, who was guilty and who was innocent.

Neither the Aldermen nor the Assistant Aldermen received any salary. The old aristocratic assumption had been that, since there was no compensation, only the most distinguished members of the community would seek these posts just for the honor of serving. The Forty Thieves made a mockery of such idealistic theory. Unpaid, they used their positions of power to feather their nests with graft.

Tweed had no compunctions. He had been an Alderman only a few weeks when he asserted his leadership among The Forty Thieves and gypped the city in a land deal that set a record for knavery at the time. The city was purchasing sixty-nine acres of land on Ward's Island for use as a Potter's Field, a burial ground for the poor. At the very highest estimate, the land was worth no more than $30,000; but Tweed, with the connivance of an unscrupulous mayor, palmed it off on the city for $103,450. The Forty Thieves had never turned such a profit before, and, with Tweed showing the way, the looting was just beginning.

Every transaction, large or small, became a crooked deal. The city spent $4,100 for Fourth of July fireworks that, at the outside, should have cost no more than $500. And the very next day, July 5, 1852, The Forty Thieves cashed in on the funeral of Henry Clay. The body of the great Kentuckian, which had been lying in state in City Hall, was to be transported by steamer to Albany. Tweed and his cohorts, the most patriotic of mourners on the surface, saw another opportunity to fleece the city. They got tradesmen to submit bills for $2,500 for decorating the little steamer with a few flags and some strips of black and white cotton bunting; they charged off $1,400 for cigars, wine, and refreshments. It was a petty and ghoulish thievery, gouging the city for its tribute to one of the great national leaders; and it demonstrated that, when even such a funeral was not sacred, all bars were down and there was no limit.

Henry Clay's funeral had been the occasion for penny ante graft, mere pocket money; but franchises were something else. The Forty Thieves licked their chops over those. A ferry franchise was hocked to the highest bidder for $20,000. Thousands of dollars (the total never was determined) were milked out of a Broadway street franchise. A sale of city land brought The Forty Thieves between $40,000 and $75,000 in bribes. Another $30,000 was reaped from a Third Avenue railway franchise. A $600,000 contract was awarded to a favorite contractor for paving the Bowery—and the paving proved so worthless it had to be ripped up almost the moment it was laid.

The looting of the public till became so colossal, so all-encompassing, that Tweed did not have time to keep track of all the deals himself, and so he named a ne'er-do-well relation of his wife to protect his interest in gathering in the plunder. Tweed himself was preoccupied with his ambitions. He aimed at acquiring ever more power and a virtually limitless illegal fortune. His first step, taken in the election of 1852, when he was only twenty-nine, was to get himself elected to the House of Representatives from the Fifth New York Congressional District. However, he continued to sit in the Common Council until January 1, 1854; the rewards there were just too juicy to give up.

Tweed did not like Congress. He soon learned that a first-term Congressman was merely tolerated in Washington. He had no real power—and little opportunity for the kind of lush pickings that were available in New York. As a result, Tweed abandoned the nation's capital after his one term and concentrated on the political struggles in his native city.

His keen mind soon told him that 1853 was a bad year for a member of The Forty Thieves. Some of the city's newspapers, outraged by the brazen freebooting, had begun to hammer at the ring; a reform tide was rising. Sensing this, Tweed refused to run for any office, and the outcome showed he had been wise. The reformers triumphed and took control of the Common Council.

What happened next is what so often happens. The reformers, once in office, proved themselves inept politicians. When they failed to carry out the more ambitious parts of the program on which they had been elected, the press turned on them, too, and an adverse public reaction began to set in. Tweed watched all of this with a cynical eye. He devoted himself to business, running his father-in-law's brush factory and his father's chairmaking establishment; but he found time to prowl constantly around the corridors of City Hall, sniffing the political winds, gathering the scuttlebutt from the lobbyists who clustered there.

Though out of politics for the moment, Tweed was studying every political move, savoring the successful techniques, preparing for the time when he would use them and become the boss. The election of 1854 was a contest between wildly split political factions. The City Reform Party had a full slate in the field. The Democrats were divided into two hostile groups. And then there were the Native Americans, or the Know Nothings, as they were called, a faction that appealed to prejudice of every kind. They were violently anti-Catholic; they stirred up the hatred of native-born Americans against foreigners and immigrants of every nationality; and by these appeals to ignorance and passion, they had gathered an enormous following and threatened to dominate the political life of the city.

Out of this turmoil came Fernando Wood. He was one of the handsomest men ever to become Mayor of New York. He was five feet eleven and slender. He had deep blue eyes and dark brown hair, and his voice, soft in ordinary conversation, was clear and resonant on the public platform. He had acquired great wealth, first from a waterfront groggery in which he bilked drunken sailors, next from a fleet of coastwise trading ships. When gold was discovered in California, one of the first vessels carrying fortune-hunting Forty-Niners from New York to San Francisco flew the house flag of Fernando Wood.

Wood had been a secret and prominent member of the Know Nothings, a tie that could well have cost him the votes of the foreign-born in the election of 1854. Wood insured himself against this disaster by forming whispering squads that made him all things to all men. In Know Nothing districts, his hirelings spread the word that he had been a member of the Know Nothings all along. In districts where the foreign-born vote was important, Wood's agents assured the voters that he had never been a Know Nothing and that this was just a vile story made up by his enemies to discredit him. With the help of this many-sided whispering campaign, with the vote split in a field of five candidates, Fernando Wood was elected mayor, although he had polled only one vote out of three.

The election of Wood enthroned corruption in New York's City Hall. The new mayor levied on everyone and everything. City employees had to kick in a percentage of their salary to Wood's kitty. Policemen were forced to contribute from $25 up, depending upon their rank. Owners of grog shops, gambling dens, and bawdy houses paid heavy bribes to insure themselves against interference by the law. Even legitimate businesses and powerful businessmen were brought to heel. Wood, through his minions, controlled the assessments of real and personal property. If merchants did not want to be taxed out of existence, they had to make their peace with Wood; if they wanted to sell supplies to city departments, they had to deal with him on his terms. Banks that obtained large city deposits and paid ridiculously low interest rates had to keep the mayor's favor—or lose their profits.

Wood marshalled all of these sources of power and put the pressure on everyone, high and low, when he faced a stiff fight for re-election in 1856. He had a glowing testimonial drawn up, picturing himself as a paragon of rectitude and his administration as the purest the city had ever seen. This nauseous document was signed, under pressure, of course, by the leading respectables of the city—bankers, merchants, large property owners. The list included even the name of William B. Astor, the son of John Jacob Astor and the head of the House of Astor with its incredible millions.

This whitewashing document helped to re-elect Fernando Wood in a split field, and soon the corruption of his first administration was being surpassed by that of his second.

Big Bill Tweed—as he was now being called—observed all this from his position in the inner circles of Tammany. He presently held a minor city post of no real power, that of School Commissioner, and supported Wood because he felt the alternative was the election of the Know Nothing candidate. And Tweed, whatever his faults, never traveled the road of racial and religious bigotry.

His support of Wood was, however, as he later confessed, one of the most distasteful acts of his life. It was not the corruption of Wood's administration that bothered him; Tweed himself was corrupt. What he saw in Wood was a powerful rival who had to be brought down if Tweed himself was to become the boss of New York. There was, Tweed knew, no limit to Wood's ambitions; he was not content just to rule the city, he looked beyond it to the state—and indeed to the White House itself. True, Tweed himself had similar ambitions, but he knew they could never be fulfilled as long as Fernando Wood stood in the way.

The year 1857, a few months after Wood's re-election, became the turning point for Tweed. The nation's economy collapsed in the panic of 1857—a disaster from which Tweed reaped considerable political benefit. Every bank in New York City closed its doors, as did banks in New England and other sections of the country. Businesses of every kind collapsed. Poverty intensified into starvation. Seacoast cities like New York were especially hard-hit. Their slums held the hundreds of thousands of immigrants who had come from Europe in the 1840s; and these newcomers, living on the ragged edge of destitution in the best of times, were now dragged down into sub-human depths. In just one ward—the Sixth, north of City Hall—charitable organizations fed 10,000 in a single day.

When such disasters strike, the poor and desperate seek help wherever they can get it. This is the golden opportunity of the political boss. If he takes care of his people in such dire circumstances, he wins their eternal gratitude—and their votes. This is just what Big Bill Tweed did. He set an example that other politicians soon followed by donating $500—a sum of much larger worth then than now —to help the starving in his Seventh Ward. And he personally saw to it that no family in his district lacked coal for heat in this harsh winter of depression. Thus his reputation as a big-hearted, generous man who looked after his own was enhanced. It was an image that he and other political bosses after him were to find invaluable.

These hard times had given Tweed the opportunity to wear a halo as the doer of good deeds; and now, in this same year of 1857, the reformers presented him with the opportunity to become boss—a position in which he could proceed to steal the public blind.

The Republican Party had been formed in the national election of 1856, bringing together under one tent the Whigs and various splinter parties opposed to slavery. The new party elected the governor of

New York and seized control of the state machinery. Once in power, it promptly turned attention to its hated foe, Tammany, and to the pervasive corruption of New York itself.

The reformers devised a plan that was supposed to purify the city. A bipartisan Board of Supervisors was created. The Common Council would remain, but the new Supervisors would have control of the election machinery and broad powers to check on corrupt deals. Six members of the new board were to be Democrats, six Republicans; and in their zeal the Republicans believed that their own six stalwarts on the board would checkmate the Democrats and insure honest government. Actually, it was impossible for them to imagine at the time that they were creating a situation which would lead ultimately to the enthronement of the Tweed Ring.

One major flaw of the reform measure was that it deprived the voters of any real choice. Party caucuses handpicked the six men on each side, and the voters could only vote for the tickets presented to them. It was an arrangement that could hardly fail to put a premium on backroom skullduggery.

Tweed saw his chance and got himself elected to this new Board of Supervisors. For the first year, it seemed as if the new bipartisan system might work; so far as could ever be discovered, there were no crooked deals. Perhaps Tweed was just biding his time.

At any rate, the election of 1858 was highly important to him. Fernando Wood was running again, and, if Tweed was to achieve power, Wood must be defeated. Some other leaders felt the same way, but for more principled reasons. One of those who was appalled by Wood's corruption and who worked quietly for his defeat was Samuel J. Tilden. Later, Tilden was to become Tweed's own nemesis and probably the only man legally elected President of the United States ever to be denied his seat.

While the attention of Tilden and others was concentrated on Wood, Tweed focused on getting his own men into positions of power lower down on the ticket. Wood was so preoccupied with himself and others were so preoccupied with Wood that nobody noticed what Tweed was doing. And so he got two of his own tools strategically placed. One was Peter B. Sweeney, whom Tweed put up for District Attorney; the other was George G. Barnard, who was nominated for Recorder, a judge with the power to try capital cases.

Sweeney and Barnard were elected, and Wood was defeated by

Daniel F. Tiemann, a member of Tammany Hall behind whom Republicans, independents, and Know Nothings all united. Even so, the mayoralty vote was close. Tiemann won by only 2,500 votes, and this margin could have been easily wiped out had Wood employed to full effect one new tactic—one Tweed would remember and make fuller use of later.

Wood had some 4,000 foreigners naturalized by friendly judges just before election day, making them new Americans in return for their votes in the ballot box. Those 4,000 extra votes could well have been 10,000 if Wood had made fuller use of this new technique, Tweed realized; and, had Wood done this, he would have won.

With the defeat of Wood, Tweed was on the threshold of supreme power. He was just thirty-five in 1858, and he was about to be known as The Boss. He had the District Attorney, a judge, the county clerk, and numerous less powerful officeholders in his hip pocket; he was building his own personal machine. And he was helped along by one great, left-over scandal from the Wood administration—one that resulted in the unprecedented sale of City Hall on the auction block.

In one of the last acts of his administration, Mayor Wood, in cahoots with the members of the Common Council, had agreed to purchase for the city a parcel of land worth no more than $60,000 for a price of $196,000. The land was owned by a Wall Street broker, Robert W. Lowber, who had only $20,000 equity in the property. When Wood was defeated, Mayor Tiemann refused to go along with the corrupt deal. Lowber sued.

He won in the courts since he had a binding contract with the city. The judgment, with interest and costs, came to $228,000. Lowber turned this over to the Sheriff to collect, and the Sheriff advertised City Hall for sale.

A horrendous possibility arose. It was rumored that Fernando Wood, with his enormous wealth, intended to buy City Hall and evict from the Mayor's office the man who had just defeated him at the polls. As it turned out, this did not happen. Wood didn't bid, and City Hall was knocked down to Mayor Tiemann for the nominal sum of $50,000. Tiemann kept title to the hall until the city eventually paid him back.

When even City Hall could be hocked on the public auction block as the outcome of a corrupt deal, little more needs to be said about the prevailing political ethics of New York. The atmosphere was ideal for the functioning of the first Tweed Ring which Big Bill put together in the fall of 1859.

The ring was founded on bribery. The innocents who had created the Board of Supervisors had assumed that the even-up, six-to-six bipartisan composition would prevent crooked dealing, but Tweed saw farther. He realized that all he needed to gain complete control was to corrupt one man among the Republican opposition. This he did. Peter B. Voorhis, a Republican coal merchant, accepted a $2,500 bribe to stay away from the vital meeting at which the Supervisors appointed election officials. His absence gave Tweed, who had engineered the deal, a six-to-five vote edge—in other words, full control. Accordingly, he supervised the appointment of 609 election inspectors, some 550 of them Democrats and a goodly portion of these saloon-keepers, gamblers, and gangsters. Into such hands, Tweed placed the power to stuff ballot boxes and to falsify the returns on election day, regardless of the will of the voters.

Despite this control of the election machinery by Tweed, Fernando Wood staged a comeback and was re-elected mayor in a three-cornered race in 1859. He began his third term in City Hall on January 1, 1860, but he was now only a shell of the all-powerful politician he once had been. Behind the scenes, the real power belonged to Tweed, and, before the year was out, he was no longer being called Bill or Big Bill, but The Boss.

As The Boss, Tweed rode roughshod over all opposition. He himself presided at party nominating conventions when he had a candidate whom he wanted endorsed for a particular post; and it did not matter to him what the majority of those present wanted. If he saw he did not have enough votes to put over his candidate, he would simply get one of his hirelings to make a motion to dispense with a roll call. As chairman of the meeting, he would then call for a voice vote; and, despite an overwhelming chorus of "Noes" that greeted the name of his candidate, Tweed would simply pound the gavel and declare his man nominated.

These tactics often infuriated the opposition, especially that notorious thug, Isaiah Rynders, who had been elevated to the position of U. S. Marshal. On one occasion, when Rynders' handpicked candidate had been gaveled into extinction by Tweed, a riot broke out and Tweed was driven into a corner. Rynders pulled a pistol and thrust it against the breast of The Boss. Tweed stared him down and told him with cold contempt: "I'm not afraid of a whole ward of your fighting villains."

It was a magnificent demonstration of courage. The glint in the steely eyes and the massive, indomitable figure of The Boss cowed even Isaiah Rynders. He put away his gun, and Tweed marched past him as if clothed in some invisible armor. The story of this encounter, as it was told and retold, added to the stature of The Boss and gave him a heroic image.

By such domineering methods, Tweed built an ever more powerful machine, one that held out to the faithful the certain promise of rich rewards. The Boss boosted complaisant Judge Barnard, who had never failed to free one of Tweed's strong-arms at Tweed's nod, to a position on the State Supreme Court. And he brought into his circle one of the most engaging personalities in the city at the time— handsome, witty A. Oakey Hall, a fashion plate who became known as The Elegant Oakey. Hall had been a Whig, a Know Nothing, a Republican; but, in the election of 1860, he turned his political coat again and became a Tweed Democrat. Tweed rewarded him by getting him elected District Attorney, a mere stepping-stone to the Mayor's office in City Hall.

With the election of Abraham Lincoln as President came the onset of the Civil War and one of the most turbulent periods New York had ever seen. The election of 1861, following the outbreak of the war, was a disaster for Tweed. He ran for Sheriff, and he poured every cent of the $100,000 he had accumulated into his campaign, only to be defeated. The outcome left him virtually bankrupt, though no one could ever have guessed it from the high-handed manner in which he continued to conduct his private and political affairs. For Tweed, there was just one consolation. Fernando Wood had been exposed during the campaign for having looted the city of at least $250,000, and he had gone down to a shattering defeat, running third in a field of three. Wood was finished. And Tweed, despite his personal defeat, was still the real power behind the scenes in municipal affairs.

He retained his seat on the all-important Board of Supervisors, and he used this strategic position to superintend the collection of graft. Years later, after his final downfall, Tweed explained the way the system worked in these words: "Pretty nearly every person who had business with the Board of Supervisors, or furnished the county with supplies, had a friend on the Board of Supervisors, and generally with some member of the Ring. And through that one member they were talked to, and the result was that their bills were sent in and passed, and the percentages were paid on the bills, sometimes to one man, sometimes to another."

These "percentages" came in time to represent staggering sums of money. The Ring began by tacking 10 per cent on every contract negotiated with the city; but by 1867, with Tweed ever more powerful and holding City Hall in a strangler's grip, these grafting "percentages" had been hiked to a shocking degree. It was understood by every contractor dealing with the city that his legitimate charges must be padded 35 per cent. This was the bribe money necessary to do business. Of this 35 per cent, Tweed kept 25 and the remaining 10 was divided among his crooked accomplices.

To keep the public from realizing just how badly it was being fleeced, Tweed devised a payoff system designed to lessen the zeal of reporters covering City Hall and the higher courts. Just a few days before Christmas, 1862, he got the Common Council to pass a bill rewarding these journalists with $200 each. The Republican Mayor who had defeated Fernando Wood vetoed the measure, but the council, with Tweed prodding it, promptly passed the brazen journalistic bribe over his veto.

Money now rolled in upon The Boss in an unending green cascade. Stony broke though he had been after the disastrous election of 1861, he replenished his bank account so swiftly that he was wealthy again by the spring of 1863, and by the end of the war, in 1865, he was a millionaire. From zero dollars to millions in just four years— what a track record! But Tweed was not alone. The war boom made crooks—and millionaires—out of almost everyone in a position to take advantage of it.

In just the first eighteen months of the war, according to caustic editor James Gordon Bennett, at least 150 New Yorkers had fattened their wallets by from $150,000 to $1,500,000 apiece. "These shoddy aristocrats," Bennett editorialized, "have added about 200 brilliant new equipages to the ring at [Central] Park and will soon figure at the watering places. Jay Cooke, the banker, cleared $300,000 by the conversion of government bonds alone."

Tweed, like all the other grafters and profiteers, rode high. Not even the bloody draft riots that almost tore the city apart in early July, 1863, shortly after the great victory at Gettysburg, tarnished his image. The Draft Act passed by the Lincoln Administration, the first measure of its kind in the nation, was doubtless necessary for the prosecution of the war, but it was so unfair and discriminatory that it touched off an outburst of fury. Under the act's provisions, the poor man had no choice; he had to let himself be drafted and marched off to war. But the rich man could be permanently excused from duty if he hired a substitute to serve in his place, or he could be exempted temporarily by paying $300. In New York City, where thousands had opposed the war from the beginning, this injustice fueled a full-scale rebellion.

Pitched battles were fought in the streets for four days. It was estimated that 1,000 persons were killed, 8,000 wounded. The homes of the wealthy were special targets. More than 100 buildings were burned and another 250 looted and damaged. Property losses were put at $2 million. Rioting mobs hanged Negroes from the lamp posts, killed three policemen, and inflicted injuries on every member of the force. The bloody insurrection was not put down until Army troops marched in and restored order, rounding up an 11,000 stand of small arms and several thousand bludgeons and other weapons used by the rioters.

Tweed, with the Elegant Oakey and Governor Horatio Seymour at his side, toured the city during the height of the riots and left no doubt where his sympathies lay. He had one of his corrupt judges rule that the Draft Act was unconstitutional, and a protestor who had been conscripted under it was set free. It was a story that made the front pages of the newspapers even as the city burned; and it was, of course, an act of demagoguery that could hardly fail to add to Tweed's popularity with the masses.

Shortly after the end of the draft riots, Tweed found for himself another and semi-legitimate road to wealth. He had himself proclaimed a lawyer. In those days, any friendly judge could admit a candidate to the bar by a simple ceremony in his chambers. It was not necessary to have any knowledge of the law—only the right pull with the right judge. No one had more pull than The Boss, and Judge Barnard, whom he had put on the bench and promoted, was only too happy to certify that Tweed could now practice law and try cases all the way up to the State Supreme Court and Court of Appeals.

Tweed promptly opened an office at 95 Duane Street, gold letters on the glass door proclaiming: "William M. Tweed, Attorney-at-

Law." Prominent businessmen were soon beating a path to this new law office. The Erie Railroad was delighted to pay Tweed more than $100,000 for his "legal advice." What such clients purchased, of course, was not Tweed's legal knowledge—he had none and never tried a case—but the influence of The Boss, camouflaged under this guise of legality.

The tide was now running Tweed's way in everything. In the municipal election of 1865, he at last realized one of his great ambitions and put one of his stooges in the Mayor's office in City Hall. The handpicked dummy was John T. Hoffman, who had made a good record as a judge but who, like Judge Barnard, had a keen sense about where the power lay and what would best serve his own self-interest.

The next five years saw Tweed at the height of his power. The payoffs were so tremendous—the Erie Railroad alone in a span of three months paid him $650,000 for his "legal advice"—that by 1870 he bragged he was worth $20 million and would soon be richer than the Vanderbilts.

With such wealth came an ever more extravagant manner of living. Tweed dined at the most fashionable and expensive places, the Astor House or Delmonico's; and no matter how many were in the party, he always picked up the tab. It was a day when men as well as women liked to wear flashy diamonds, if only to demonstrate just how much they had made, and Tweed decorated his shirt front with a blue-white gem the size of a small cherry.

This high-flying style brought changes in his family life. The family home was moved from the East Side, ever more crowded with immigrants, to a fashionable brownstone at 41 West 36th Street on the fringe of the world of high society. At the same time, Tweed removed himself more and more from his family. His children were growing up; they and his wife had their own carriages; and they often spent weekends at nearby resorts. Tweed spent the same weekends—and much of the time in between—in the company of a little blonde many years younger than himself.

When gossip began to get around town about this affair, Tweed decided that a little discretion was in order. Some of his old friends who had belonged to the volunteer fire company that had given him his start in politics had formed a social club. They called it the Americus Club, adopting the name of the old fire company. In warm weather, these companionable spirits would sail up Long Island Sound to Greenwich, Connecticut. There they would spend a week-end, camping on the beach in tents, catching fish in the sound, gathering clams and shellfish and cooking them over driftwood fires.

Tweed had joined this jovial band before he became enamored of his little blonde, and when he learned that his love affair was beginning to be talked about, it occurred to him that Greenwich would be a perfect spot in which to hide his charmer. Tweed had already made himself the dominant figure of the Americus Club and had changed its routine. Not for him the roughing it in tents pitched on the beach. Under his guidance, the club obtained a pretentious club-house directly on the sound, with a dock out front to which Tweed's yacht was moored. A symbol of club membership was a tiger's head made of gold, its eyes set with rubies. This little bauble cost $2,000, just one indication of the manner in which Tweed had turned a casual group into a swank, social-climbing organization. It was one, in any event, that now served Tweed's ends perfectly. He had a house built on property near the club, passing it off as the home of his coachman. It was, of course, the hideaway for his blonde, and The Boss continued to enjoy all the pleasures of his affair without creating the kind of scandal that could have touched off a damaging political backfire in New York.

With his personal affairs arranged so satisfactorily, Tweed now set out to grab the kind of complete power in the state that he already exercised in the city. In the election of 1867, he ran for the State Senate. The results showed his power. His stooge, Mayor Hoffman, was re-elected by an overwhelming margin, and Tweed himself outpolled his nearest competitor by nearly two to one.

Once in Albany, Tweed quickly made himself the behind-the-scenes boss of the capital. Lobbyists soon learned that, when they wanted a favorable bill enacted or a hostile one killed, the place to go was not the corridors of the State House, but a royal suite in the Delevan House where Boss Tweed presided. Tweed rented seven spacious rooms on the second floor of this hotel. Two inner rooms, a bedroom and a conference room, were reserved for his own private use. The other rooms were fitted out with sideboards glistening with cut glass and burdened with decanters of whiskey, brandy, Holland gin, and other potions guaranteed to induce a glow. Potted plants and vases of cut flowers were tastefully arranged throughout the suite, and from numerous cages, yellow canaries warbled sweetly. The Boss liked canaries.

Entrance to this lavish lair was strictly regulated. Guards stood at the outer door, and the only persons allowed to enter were those who had business with The Boss or one of his aides. In the inner conference room, Tweed presided like a king. Legislators of every persuasion quickly learned that their fate was in his hands. A legislator, if he were to please his constituents, had to get bills passed to dredge a waterway, or build a bridge, or cut through a new highway. None of this could be done without Tweed's approval. Legislators came to his throne-room hat in hand, and more often than not they got what they wanted. For these services, Tweed usually charged nothing. He greeted his visitors jovially, smiling, clasping their hands, back-slapping, and pressing upon them their choice of the liquid jollification waiting on the sideboards. Big, generous Bill Tweed was not, naturally, doing all of this out of the goodness of his heart. He had a political objective in mind—to promote Mayor Hoffman into the Governor's office in Albany. And, beyond that, who knew? Perhaps the Presidency?

While he was piling up such political IOUs for future collection, Tweed was simultaneously organizing into an efficient system what had previously been a hit-or-miss pattern of corruption. Nothing now was left to chance; there was a scale, a bribe, for everything. Legislators were organized like drill teams until these legions of the totally corrupted became known as The Black Horse Cavalry. The most powerful businesses in the state, railroads, manufacturing concerns, corporations of every stripe, had to come to The Black Horse Cavalry —and pay—for even the slightest favor they wanted from Albany.

The stink of corruption was everywhere, but Tweed ploughed ahead like some irresistible force of nature. He had his pawn, Mayor Hoffman, nominated for governor in 1868, and he put up another pawn, The Elegant Oakey, to succeed Hoffman in City Hall.

Hoffman was in trouble from the start. Studies of public opinion showed that the upstate Republican vote against Hoffman was likely to be so huge it would swamp whatever margins Tweed was able to pile up for his man in Democratic New York City. Desperate, determined to elect Hoffman no matter how he had to do it, The Boss now had recourse to the strategy of naturalizing foreigners that Fernando Wood had invented.

Wood hadn't been far-sighted enough to make maximum use of this fraudulent device, but Tweed exploited it to the full. His judicial tool, Judge Barnard, established a naturalization mill in the Supreme Court. In the preceding twelve years, immigrants had been naturalized at an average of about 6,000 a year; but now, in just twenty days, Barnard made new citizens—and new voters—out of 60,000!

Even with this wholesale fraud working for him, Tweed left nothing to chance. For the first time in an election, he made use of the telegraph to keep himself advised of the number of votes he must steal. He wired Democrats in every town and city of the state, demanding estimates of the total vote the instant the polls closed. With this data in hand, he could gauge how much he would have to pad the returns from corrupt election boards in the city to insure the election of Hoffman. Tweed didn't give the voters a chance. He fixed the returns to his liking, boosting Hoffman into the governor's chair in Albany and plunking down The Elegant Oakey Hall as Hoffman's successor as mayor.

The first of January, 1869, found Tweed enthroned as the most powerful boss in the nation's history. The city and state governments were his captive creatures; and power whetted his appetite for more power. He looked ahead. If he could re-elect Hoffman in 1870, if he could build him up sufficiently, he could perhaps in the end get his stooge elected President of the United States.

Supreme power brought supreme corruption. The looting had been bad enough before, but it was only a pale shadow to what took place now. The tale of the building of the New York County Courthouse was typical. Originally, the new courthouse was to have been constructed for $250,000. Year after year, more money was appropriated until the cost of the $250,000 building was raised to $6 million. Once the structure was completed, a new round of pillaging began. The courthouse had to be plastered inside, didn't it? It had to have plumbing. It had to be furnished. Corrupt contractors submitted bills like these: $2.5 million for acres of plastering; $1,508,410.89 for plumbing; and $4,829,426.26 just for carpets—a sum that would have purchased enough carpeting to cover most of the city. Before the Tweed Ring finished milking this gold mine, some $14 million had found its way into various pockets.

Nor was the public till the only till that was looted. Railroads were huge money-makers in those days when they were the new and virtually the only form of fast land transportation. And so the political thieves and the corporate thieves now joined hands. Tweed and his principal aides cooperated with Jay Gould and James Fisk Jr. in swindling the Erie Railroad. They forced out Cornelius Vanderbilt and Daniel Drew, and Erie board meetings began to be held in the plush retreat Fisk had set up for his beautiful mistress, Josie Mansfield. Tweed often dined with Fisk and the others in Josie's establishment, and here the conspirators put through many of the corrupt deals that looted the Erie in the same fashion that Tweed was looting the city. Fisk tapped the Erie treasury for $820,000 to buy an opera house; and, in just three years, the Erie paid out $1.5 million in bribes, camouflaged as "legal expenses."

With the buccaneers of such enterprises flashing diamonds and strutting mistresses all over town, secrecy became impossible. Almost everyone with any knowledge of public affairs knew perfectly well what was going on; and there were some rumblings, veiled hints, a few hit-and-run newspaper attacks—none of it determined enough or forceful enough to cause The Boss a moment's worry. For Tweed had his own methods of keeping the lid on the bubbling pot.

He had discovered that most of the newspapers of the day could be corrupted just as easily as the politicians. At one point, he had eighty-seven journals on his payroll, buying their silence with advertising. Between January 1, 1869 and the first half of 1871, the Tweed Ring paid New York City newspapers alone $2,703,308.48 out of the city treasury. It was also necessary to buy the silence of the press in Albany regarding the swindles in the State legislature. One paper published in the capital had received just $5,000 in advertising in 1868; under Tweed's rule, the sum soared to $207,900 in 1871.

But where, it might be asked, was the political opposition? With Democratic Tammany so corrupt under Tweed's regime, what were the Republicans doing with this golden opportunity for exposure and the making of political hay? They were doing precisely nothing. The reason: their leaders were in Tweed's hip pocket, sharing in the bribes and the loot. The New York County Republican Committee was so much under Tweed's control that, at one point, fifty-nine of its leaders were on his payroll!

There was, it seemed, no way of stopping Tweed. The election of 1870 was another triumph for him. Hoffman was re-elected governor. The Democrats swept the city and state. And Tweed, suddenly posing as a reformer, introduced in the legislature a new charter for New York City. It freed the city from state supervision and gave it home rule. This was a highly popular measure, but those who cheered Tweed as the champion of home rule did not realize at first the hidden jokers in his new charter. It gave the current mayor—Tweed's Elegant Oakey Hall—the power to appoint the heads of all city departments for terms ranging from four to eight years. In other words, no matter what might happen in an election, even if the Ring were to be overthrown, the Ring would still have its talons fastened deep into the city's hide.

With realization of what was at stake, reformers began to stir, opposition mounted. But Tweed bulldozed the new charter through the legislature by his usual method—wholesale bribery. He later testified that he had passed out $600,000 in bribes; he had purchased six Republicans leaders for $40,000 apiece. The adoption of the charter, the manner in which Tweed rode roughshod over all opposition demonstrated that he was now, in early 1871, at the very peak of his power; and it was just at this time, just when he seemed invulnerable, that events began to conspire to bring about his downfall.

The swift and bewildering overthrow of The Boss was largely attributable to the efforts of three men: Thomas Nast, the famous cartoonist who possessed one of the most savage pens the art has ever known; George Jones, the incorruptible editor of *The New York Times;* and Samuel J. Tilden, the powerful state Democratic leader who had long been appalled by Tweed's thievery and who had been restrained for too long from attacking him out of reasons of party loyalty.

Nast was the first in the field. As early as the campaign of 1868, he had drawn a savage cartoon based on the courthouse swindle. It showed Mayor Hoffman on one side of a four-fold screen behind which thieves were looting a strong box labeled "City Treasury." Above one group of looters was a sign reading "Court House." Over the top of the cartoon appeared the legend: "Thou Shalt Steal As Much As Thou Canst." And at the bottom appeared the signature: "The Ring."

This was just the opening salvo. Week after week, in *Harper's* magazine, Nast attacked Tweed, picturing him as a gross, big-bellied creature wallowing in his ill-gotten gains—a ringmaster who controlled a bloody, ferocious tiger representing Tammany Hall. These

Nast cartoons created images that live on in our minds today. Tweed was the original of the beefy, oily, cigar-smoking backroom manipulator we so often envision when we think of the political boss, and the tiger has remained as the symbol of a vicious and corrupt Tammany Hall.

Effective as Nast was, he could not have brought about the downfall of Tweed without the help of Jones and Tilden. Perhaps the worst break Tweed ever got came in the late summer of 1870 when J. B. Taylor died. Taylor had been one of the three directors of *The New York Times*—and he had been at the same time Tweed's partner in the New York Printing Company and hence Tweed's companion in corruption. As long as he lived, the columns of *The Times* were muted.

With Taylor's death, however, the picture changed. George Jones, the editor of *The Times,* had long wanted to follow the lead of Nast. He felt that a daily newspaper could keep up a steady fire on the Ring and be even more effective than *Harper's.* Freed at last, he loosed an opening editorial blast at the Ring on September 20, 1870. The editorial began: "We should like to have a treatise from Mr. Tweed in the art of growing rich in as many years as can be counted on the fingers of one hand. It would be instructive to young men as an example and a warning. . . . You begin with nothing and in five or six years you can boast of your ten millions. How is it done?" It was a basic and brutal question.

Nast and Jones complemented each other in the journalistic world, but more was needed—a political leader who could weld together the opposition, who could give official weight and authority to the attack. Such a leader was Tilden.

His role was perhaps more important—and, at the same time, less admirable—than the parts played by Nast and Jones. An upright man himself, Tilden had hesitated as one of state's leading Democrats to break openly with a boss of his own party who commanded the votes and the power that Tweed did. But the devious Tweed charter of 1870 had been too much for Tilden. He had opposed it. He and Tweed had clashed openly and bitterly, and Tilden, outraged, became at last a determined foe.

Such was the situation when the thieves fell out. Jimmy O'Brien, who often consulted with Tilden, was finishing a term as Sheriff in 1871. His legitimate fees had been huge, but the sight of the Tweed

Ring rolling in millions had made him greedy. He put in a bill for "extras" totaling $250,000. Tweed's Board of Audit refused to pay it. O'Brien threatened blackmail; unless he got his extra quarter of a million dollars, he said, he would publish the fraudulent bills that had been paid by the City Comptroller, Richard B. Connolly, a key figure in the Ring.

Matters were deadlocked—O'Brien threatening, the Ring refusing to pay—when the city auditor died. O'Brien by some devious maneuvering managed to wangle a friend of his, W. S. Copeland, into Comptroller Connolly's office to do the bookkeeping. Copeland made a copy of records showing fraudulent payments running into millions of dollars and turned these documents over to O'Brien. O'Brien, in turn, took them to George Jones, of *The Times*. They were a heaven-sent gift to Jones. Here was proof, taken from the city's own ledgers, to substantiate the charges of corruption that he had been making for months. Beginning in July, 1871, and continuing throughout the summer, *The Times* ran a steady barrage of articles exposing the wholesale looting by the Tweed Ring.

Even Tweed and his hardened political rogues now began to squirm. They sought to silence the opposition as they had done so often before—with money. Comptroller Connolly went to Jones and offered him $5 million to abandon his exposé of the Ring; Nast was offered $500,000 to forget all and go off on an unlimited tour of Europe. Tweed's career had been built upon the proposition that every man has his price; all that is necessary is to find the right price. It was a philosophy that had always worked in the past, but, unfortunately for Tweed and the Ring, they had come up against two honest men—men who wouldn't sell out for any price.

Tweed was so furious he would have liked to kill, but he did not dare. Nast's increasingly savage cartoons pierced even his hardened hide. "I don't care what people write," he said once, "for my people can't read. But they have eyes and they can see as well as other folks."

For a time, Tweed tried to weather the storm by putting on a show of brazen defiance. When a *Times* reporter sought to question him, he did not deny anything. He simply demanded truculently: "What are you going to do about it?"

Tilden, though he had long known about the corruption, had thought at first that *The Times'* figures regarding the enormity of the looting must be exaggerated. But when there was no response, when

The Times dared Tweed and others it had named to sue for libel—
and they didn't—Tilden became convinced. In September, 1871, he
sent out his customary call to 26,000 Democratic leaders across the
state to pick delegates to the state convention of the party; and, with
this, he threw down the gauntlet of battle to Tweed. He wrote:
"Wherever the gangrene of corruption has reached the Democratic
Party, we must take a knife and cut it out by the roots."

The mounting pressures became too severe for Comptroller Connolly. He decided to desert the sinking Tweed Ring and tried to make
his peace with Tilden. Tilden refused to represent him as a lawyer,
but persuaded Connolly not to resign. He also induced the quaking
comptroller to appoint A. H. Green as his deputy, with custody of all
financial documents. By this move, Tilden gained new access to official records that proved the knavery of the Ring.

Green discovered that huge payoffs had been funneled through
accounts in the National Broadway Bank; and, in his official capacity
as Connolly's deputy, he asked Tilden to examine the records. Tilden
was happy to oblige. With two assistants, he spent ten days tracking
down various bank transactions, and this is what he discovered: Contractors on the courthouse project had been paid by the city from an
account in the bank, then they had funneled a set percentage of the
money they received to a go-between, and the go-between had deposited these kickbacks in the accounts of members of the Ring.
Tweed had been so confident these transactions would never be discovered that he had allowed his split-ups to be deposited in an account in his name as they accrued. The total bills submitted by just
two contractors on the courthouse project had come to $6,312,000.
From one contractor, Tweed had received a kickback of 24 per cent;
from the other, one of 42 per cent. Tilden set forth his findings in an
affidavit entitled: "Figures That Could Not Lie."

On October 26, 1871, Tilden gave his findings to the newspapers, and this exposure, coming on top of the constant hammering by
Nast and Jones, sparked one of those rare bursts of public outrage. A
reform movement gathered steam, and in the municipal election of
1871, the reformers were swept into office by overwhelming majori-
ties. Only Tweed managed to swim against the tide. He still controlled
the election machinery in his district, and he stole enough votes to
gain re-election to the State Senate. But his victory was a hollow one.
He had been so crushed by Tilden's devastating attack that he did not

dare take his seat; he did not dare any longer to face his accusers. During his entire term, his Senate seat remained vacant—a mute testimonial of the extent to which The Boss had been discredited.

The Ring now began to fall apart, its members acting on the principle that he who loves himself best saves himself first. Peter B. Sweeney, who had been one of Tweed's principal lieutenants, fled to Canada and then on to Paris. Comptroller Connolly, who, like Sweeny, had some $6 million in pocket cash, took his loot and fled abroad—and, ultimately, died there. Lesser officials vanished like rats swimming from a sinking ship; still others were indicted, tried, and sent to prison. Finally, in late 1871, The Boss himself was indicted on 120 counts charging felony, forgery, grand larceny, false pretenses, and conspiracy to defraud.

This was the beginning of a years-long legal struggle for Tweed. After a long and complicated first trial at which Tilden was the star witness, a jury disagreed about Tweed's guilt. Free on bail, Tweed then fled to California. He was brought back and tried a second time, and this time he was convicted and sentenced to twelve years in prison. He was held in jail pending his appeal, and on December 4, 1875, he gave his custodians the slip in a mysterious disappearance. Tweed himself later said that this vanishing act cost him $60,000. He hid out for a time, then traveled to Florida and over to Cuba. From there, he sailed for Spain.

He might have escaped except for one fact: Nast's cartoons pursued him to the end. The artist, in a savage attack on Tweed, had drawn for *Harper's* magazine a cartoon with the central figure—a gross caricature of Tweed—clad in prison stripes. When American officials asked Spain to apprehend Tweed, Spanish soldiers were given a copy of Nast's cartoon. They could not read English but they studied the features Nast had drawn so well, and when they boarded the sailing ship that had brought Tweed to Vigo, they had little trouble identifying a sailor whom they found swabbing the decks as the fugitive Boss of New York.

Tweed's health was now breaking. The pressures of the years, the tensions of trial and pursuit had taken their toll. He was suffering from diabetes, and his heart was giving out. Brought back to New York, confined in the Ludlow Steet jail, he realized that he did not have much longer to live, and he began to long for just one boon above all others. He wanted to breathe free air again; he wanted to avoid the disgrace of dying in prison. And so he sought a deal. He would tell all in return for his release.

Now, suddenly, New York officialdom at every level was not so eager to learn all Tweed might have to tell. Some, yes—but *all?* The corruption Tweed had fathered had been state-wide. It had embraced, not just the notorious members of his Ring, but many officials, both Republicans and Democrats, who had waxed fat on the crooked deals he had engineered and who were still, many of them, important figures in the political life in several upstate cities. Who knew where Tweed's *all* might lead?

The result was that the state gingerly accepted a statement made by Tweed, and he was called to give some limited testimony before an Aldermanic investigating committee. But the lid was kept on; Tweed was never given the opportunity to tell all. Even Peter B. Sweeney was allowed to come back from Paris and settle out of court by returning to the city only a small fraction of the millions he had stolen. Tweed had offered to testify against Sweeney, but the out-of-court settlement, so small and so suspect, spared officials the possibly embarrassing necessity of using Tweed. A flat promise that had been made to him that he would be released from jail in return for his testimony was broken.

Tweed remained in prison, suffering from increasingly frequent heart attacks. On April 3, 1878, he celebrated his fifty-fifth birthday at a small dinner with some friends in the warden's quarters. Nine days later, stricken with a final heart attack, he died.

He had been the first and one of the most powerful of all American bosses. He had masterminded the looting of the public till to a degree that still staggers the imagination. An accountant who tracked down all available records estimated that the Tweed Ring in those last three and a half years had stolen between $45 and $50 million. Other estimates ranged all the way up to $200 million. And this was just for the city alone; no attempt was ever made to determine what the corruption in Albany had cost.

William Marcy Tweed had not only been the first of the great political bosses, but his career had illustrated two basic truths about the American political-boss system. The first is that it operates on a double standard. When Tweed was questioned about his conduct in bribing

Republican Supervisor Voorhis, the deed that gave him control of the election machinery, he stoutly defended his action. Pressed to admit that the bribe was improper, he replied:

"Oh, no! I don't think men are governed in these matters by ideas of what would be [in civil life] between man and man. I have never known a party man who wouldn't take advantage of such a circumstance."

It was significant, not only that Tweed made such a statement, but that no one challenged it. And it was significant, too, that he was expressing and defending a double standard that exists today, a hundred years later, just as it did then.

In a political life in which it is held honorable to disregard standards of honor between man and man, a political life in which any tactic that wins is held justifiable and not unethical, it was perhaps not surprising that Tweed's final offer to tell *all* should have been received, not with eagerness, but with apprehension. Even the highest officials—even Tilden, who was then governor and was soon, had the count been honest, to be elected President over Rutherford B. Hayes —obviously dreaded what that *all* might reveal. And so it was never told. This, too, is a basic fact of American political life. Exposures of corruption always, infallibly, end with a few scapegoats who are too obviously and deeply involved to be exculpated. But that is as far as the process ever goes. When corruption has run rampant on the Tweed scale, it is safer not to have a Tweed tell *all,* for that *all* almost certainly would involve too many and too much.

Honorable Fernando Wood, Mayor of New York City.

Samuel J. Tilden.

William M. (Boss) Tweed.

"What are you laughing at? To the victor belong the spoils."
Cartoon by Thomas Nast.

" 'The Upright Bench,' which is above criticism."
Cartoon by Thomas Nast.

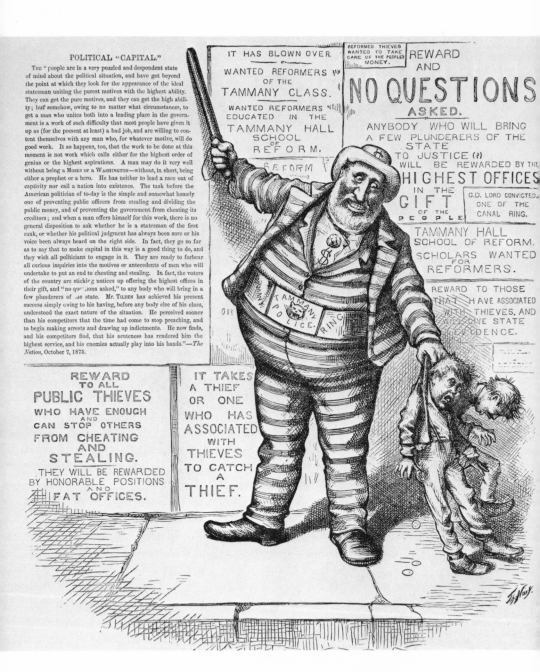

The Thomas Nast cartoon that was used by Spanish soldiers to identify Boss Tweed.

4

---◆·◆---

Mark Hanna,
the Kingmaker

H E WAS A different type of political boss—a millionaire businessman who gave up business and turned to politics; a man who
became the kingmaker, who almost single-handedly made his protege
President of the United States. He was the closest America has ever
come to having a national political boss.

His name was Marcus Alonzo Hanna. He had been born to business, and business throughout his life remained his god. He fully believed that what was good for the cash register was good for the country, and he built up the image of the Republican Party as the party of
prosperity and "the full dinner pail." He instituted a new type of regime, with millionaire businessmen actually running the affairs of
government, effecting a marriage of government and business; and
hence his influence was to last far beyond his own lifetime—down to
the Great Depression of 1929 and the Presidential election of 1932.

Mark Hanna, as he was known, was born in New Lisbon, Ohio,
on September 24, 1837. His was the richest family in town. His
grandfather, Benjamin Hanna, had founded a prosperous wholesale
and retail grocery business. Benjamin and his tall, muscular, imposing
sons not only owned the store but much of the best land in the area, a
flour mill, and other interests. Benjamin Hanna was often referred to
respectfully as "Squire."

The Hannas were a robust lot. When Squire Benjamin and his

sons argued, according to New Lisbon legend at least, you could hear their voices two miles away. The most intelligent and best educated of the sons was Leonard, a tall slender man with long-fingered, delicate hands. He had studied in the East and been trained as a doctor, but a fall from a horse in early manhood injured his spine and put an end to his career in medicine. Unable to practice, he settled down in New Lisbon and devoted himself to business interests and his family. He was the father of Mark Hanna.

As a boy, little Mark must have listened to one of the crucial business debates of the times. New Lisbon was a busy town, but new systems of transportation were changing American life. Canals were the marvel of the age—and then, of course, there was that new-fangled thing called the railroad. New Lisbon, if it was to keep growing, must establish a link by one means or another with the outside commercial world. But which means should it chose? The Hannas plumped for a canal that would link the town with the Great Lakes on the one hand and Pittsburgh on the other. Some $200,000 of the family fortune was sunk into the digging of this ditch, which was never to be of any use, for the railroads quickly made canals archaic. And the new rail networks bypassed New Lisbon, casting a blight upon its future prospects. In 1852, therefore, Dr. Leonard Hanna and his brother, Robert, took what money they could salvage from the wreckage and moved to Cleveland, where they opened a new wholesale grocery business.

The advantages of wealth—and its attendant risks—were thus bred into Mark Hanna's being from his earliest boyhood. He was a rosy-cheeked boy, big for his age, bouncing with vitality. He was decidedly no intellectual. While the family lived in New Lisbon, he attended grammar school in the basement of the Presbyterian Church; and, after the move to Cleveland, he went to Central High, where John D. Rockefeller, the future Standard Oil tycoon, was one of his classmates. The evidence says that Mark Hanna had no taste for books and study; in fact, he was twenty before he struggled through Central High in a class with boys two to four years younger.

His father, still hoping to strike an intellectual spark somewhere, enrolled him in Western Reserve University in Cleveland, but Mark did not last long there. He was soon expelled for a boyish prank that the faculty did not appreciate. Dr. Leonard Hanna didn't appreciate it either. Feeling that the family had been disgraced, he ordered his son to apologize to his mother for his conduct. It was an edict that brought to the fore one of the most prominent traits in Mark Hanna's character—a mule-like stubbornness.

Mark was by this time a stocky, thick-chested, large-shouldered young man. He had huge, alert brown eyes set in a freckled, squarish face dominated by a granite jaw. When he set that jaw, nothing could move him; and he set it now. He would *not* apologize to his mother, the former Samantha Converse. Nor did he. Contrarily, Samantha rather liked his obstinacy. She had come west from Vermont at a time when going west was still an adventure; she had much of the spirit of the pioneering woman in her; and she had no respect at all for men who submitted meekly, who "gave in."

In this respect, at least, she did not have to worry about her son; but there was the problem, since he obviously had no taste for education, of what to do with him. Fortunately, there was the booming Hanna business, thanks in large measure to the vision of Dr. Leonard Hanna. In 1853, shortly after coming to Cleveland, Mark's father had gone on a sailing trip up the lakes for his health. He had seen the eagerness with which isolated wilderness hamlets greeted the arrival of his ship, and he had come back fired with an inspiration. A steamboat fleet traveling up and down the Great Lakes, carrying supplies to towns still sunk in the wilderness, bringing back pig-iron, salted fish, timber and furs, would make money. Cautious Robert Hanna objected, but the imaginative Leonard had his way; the vessels were built, trade boomed. And so now there was a place for Mark Hanna in an expanding business.

He put on overalls and worked as a stevedore on the company docks. He was a physical man, and his muscles responded with joy. He delighted in activity and was never happier than when he was swapping yarns with the roustabouts or sailing as a purser on the family steamers on their trips up the lakes. In the process, of course, he was learning every detail of the various businesses so important to the Hanna family.

This knowledge became important in 1861 when the Civil War broke out. The Hannas had been ardent supporters of Abraham Lincoln, the first Republican President, and Mark felt that, since they had backed Lincoln, he ought to go off to Lincoln's war. But his mother vetoed the idea emphatically—and for a very good reason. She knew that his father was slowly dying; and aside from the family business, there was no family fortune. With Dr. Hanna unable to carry on, Mark was needed at home to safeguard the family interests. Rebellious and stubborn as usual, Mark Hanna knew nevertheless that she was right; and so this time he yielded, staying behind in Cleveland and feeling guilty when he saw his friends march off to fight.

His surrender to his mother's wishes had one compensation. He met *the* girl. She was Charlotte Augusta Rhodes, tall, slim and attractive, fresh from a New York finishing school. Her father was Daniel Rhodes, one of the wealthiest men in Cleveland, a coal and iron baron. There was just one drawback: Daniel Rhodes was an ardent Democrat, and he blustered and fumed at the thought of his adored daughter's marrying a young Republican.

It is the history of such affairs that obstinate fathers usually yield in the end to their even more obstinate daughters, and so it was in this case. On September 27, 1864, Charlotte Rhodes and Mark Hanna were married. It was to prove a happy union for both—and an especially fortunate one for Mark Hanna, for he had married into an industrial empire far greater than his own, and he was to need that buffer.

As the Civil War ended, bumptious and over-confident Mark Hanna caught oil fever. The petroleum industry was just beginning to come into its own, and Cleveland, where John D. Rockefeller was soon to gain a monopoly, was the site of the first large refineries. Envisioning great wealth, Mark Hanna built himself one of those first large refineries. He also expanded in other directions, constructing the *Lac La Belle,* the swiftest and best-appointed lake steamer of the day. Then the blow fell. The refinery burned down; the steamer sank. Mark Hanna had no insurance on either. He had over-extended himself, and he woke up at the age of thirty to find himself broke.

His wife took him home to her father. Daniel Rhodes could not resist the "I-told-you-so," but Mark was now family and so a man to be looked after. Daniel took him into his own coal and iron business, and, though the chafing that went on must have galled Mark Hanna, he swallowed his pride and buckled down to the task of learning the intricacies of his new trade. He learned so well that when Daniel Rhodes retired shortly afterwards he was made a partner in Rhodes and Company—the firm that he was later to make famous as M. A. Hanna and Company, the cornucopia that poured out seemingly endless millions.

During the ten years between his thirtieth and fortieth birthdays, Mark Hanna was all business, and his businesses were infinitely varied. He bought and ran a newspaper; he organized and headed a bank; he owned a fleet of steamers and went into shipbuilding; he owned the Cleveland Opera House; he became one of the two leading street-railway magnates of Cleveland. In these enterprises, he did not gamble with the public's money through the sale of stock as so many entrepreneurs of his time did; all were financed with funds generated by his own businesses—and all succeeded because Mark Hanna was an astute and highly capable businessman.

With his varied interests, his mushrooming wealth, he became a figure of note in Cleveland. Residents of the city became accustomed to the sight of him walking about the Public Square, stopping to converse with business acquaintances, and pounding his walking stick vigorously upon the sidewalk to emphasize his very decided opinions. His workers, too, saw more of him than most laborers in the vineyards of big business. With the growth of huge corporations, management was becoming more and more remote from the hired hands. But not at Hanna's company. It was by no means unusual to find him strolling the docks, talking to foremen and roustabouts, a big cigar clenched between his teeth. If the discussion warranted, he would sit down upon an upturned keg, not bothering about the stain to the seat of his trousers, and there thrash out the problem that interested him.

There was an earthy wisdom about him, and he often broke with the ritual beliefs of his moneyed class. "Up to his neck a man is worth only the price of a day's labor" became one of his most famous sayings. He respected brains, but not wealth for wealth's sake. Thomas Beer, years after Hanna's death, recounted this anecdote: A man possessed of many millions but a paucity of brains was dining with Hanna one day when the richest man in the nation walked past their table, nodded, and spoke. The millionaire was thrilled; he wanted to cement a closer acquaintance with the richest man at once. But Hanna only grunted contemptuously and said he wasn't worth meeting. The mere millionaire was shocked. "Why, he's worth $200 millions," he said, referring to the mighty one. "Yes," Mark Hanna replied, "and what else is he worth?"

Unlike many of his peers, Hanna did not believe in grinding down the workingman. Business was his god, and profit the driving purpose of his life; but he felt that his workers, even when they did not have much above the neck, were at least entitled to a livelihood. This conviction was later to set him apart from most of the business monarchs of his time when one of the worst depressions in history prostrated the nation in 1873.

Meanwhile, the Civil War had touched off a wild boom that changed many fundamentals of American life. In a few short years, the agrarianism of the past began to be swept aside by the onrush of industrialization, a process that has continued at accelerated pace ever since. Big business had learned how to such the yolk from the egg of the federal treasury in Washington. Railroads had been granted baronial tracts of land in return for their skill and swiftness in threading the continent with iron rails. However, these ventures, hailed as the product of the free enterprise system, had in reality been nothing of the sort. They had been underwritten—and more than underwritten —by the federal government; and the promoters, without risking a dime of their own money, had floated huge blocks of stock, in many instances bilking the public.

Then on September 19, 1873, in the short space of seven hours, the bubble burst. Jay Cooke, one of the shadier financiers of his time, failed the day before—and Wall Street tumbled after him. Supposedly solid businesses fell into ruins, and banks crashed. Panic swept the nation—the Panic of '73. Almost one-third of all the railroads went into receivership, and farms of ninety acres could not be mortgaged for $100. Stock certificates were found abandoned in gutters, and men who had fancied themselves wealthy committed suicide by jumping from windows. Victims sat on the curb of Wall Street (the exchange had closed), and muttered to themselves that it was the end of the world.

Mark Hanna snorted his contempt of such faint hearts. He traveled far and wide, drumming up business for his coal company. He had an uncanny knack, even in the worst of times, for sniffing out where a contract might be obtained. Oftentimes competitors, catching the same scent, would rush after the same business, only to find burly Mark Hanna coming out of an office with the contract already in his pocket.

Trying to avert trouble in the mines, Hanna formed an operators' association. His hope was to get both mine owners and workers to act sensibly. He wanted the owners to pledge not to cut wages, the miners not to strike. He was convinced, as his son later wrote, "that some corporations and large industrial concerns were deliberately bleeding their workmen as a matter of selfish economy." Hanna hoped to stop the practice, but he failed. The depression deepened, and in the spring of 1876, mine operators cut wages to 65 cents a ton for coal mined in the Massillon district. These were starvation wages, and the miners struck. Disorders broke out; the mine owners appealed to the governor for help. A company of state militia was sent into the coal region, and the strikers responded by setting fire to two mines of Rhodes and Company. Mark Hanna was furious. Striding into his home that night, he threw his hat the length of the hallway and exclaimed: "God damn militia, anyhow!"

As head of the operators' association, Hanna had to do his best to see that charges brought against twenty-three miners arrested in the disturbances were not dropped. He had little stomach for the task since he was out of sympathy with the actions that had produced the crisis. The situation of the arrested men was truly desperate. The violence in the mines had led to a hysterical public reaction, and no lawyer wanted to defend the jailed men. But in the end such a man finally came forward; and the fact that he did, though Hanna couldn't recognize it at the time, marked a turning point in his own career.

William McKinley had gone into the Union Army during the Civil War as a volunteer, a buck private in the ranks, and had risen to become a major. He was a handsome man, with charming manners and an appealing, fluent voice. He was mild-mannered, never giving offense to anyone, but he could be stubborn. He was stubborn now. His friends begged him not to touch the miners' case. A political future was opening before him; he was soon to run for Congress. Why jeopardize it all? McKinley thought the men should be properly defended; and since no one else would do the job, he felt that he must. The miners were at first suspicious of him; he was too handsome, too smooth, obviously a tool who would sell them out in the end. But McKinley persisted, and won their confidence. When the case came to trial, he got all but one of them acquitted, picturing them as the small and helpless men who had become the victims of a vicious system.

This was Mark Hanna's first brushing contact, unheeded at the time, with the man who ultimately he was to make President of the United States.

In fact, Hanna had not yet become interested in politics. He sometimes muttered and stormed about local issues in Cleveland, about the condition of the streets or bad lighting on Euclid Avenue. However, once such minor grievances fixed themselves in his mind, he would harp on them in his stubborn way until he made himself a bore. Friends in the upper-crust society of Cleveland in which he moved took the attitude that politics was a dirty business and should be left to the politicians; and Mark Hanna, grumbling, went along with this reasoning—until politics began to interfere with his business. Then Hanna began to take a decided interest in politics.

An old-fashioned horsecar street railway was the instrumentality of this change. When Daniel Rhodes died in 1875, Hanna took over full management of his wife's interests in her father's estate. Among the subsidiary holdings was a fifteen-mile horsecar line that ran over a viaduct to the Public Square in Cleveland.

Elias Sims, an old steamboatman, had been Rhodes's partner in the line and was president of the company. Like all utilities, the railway depended upon franchises granted by the city fathers, and local officials, in Cleveland as elsewhere, had early learned that here was a fine source of graft. Franchises could be granted for a price, and competing franchises could be denied—for a price. Elderly Elias Sims, in his struggle to keep on the right side of the city council, had found that he had to keep passing out cash. "All the councilmen want is money," he growled. "Have to go around with my pocketbook in my hand all the time."

Mark Hanna, becoming a director of the line, didn't like such holdups. He was also disturbed by the success of a dangerous competitor. This was Tom L. Johnson—a huge, portly, generous-minded man, idealistic and with an inexhaustible supply of energy. Beginning in his youth with a single horsecar, he had built up a prosperous streetcar line, the largest in Cleveland. But his idealism had set his feet on a path that diverged sharply from Mark Hanna's. Johnson had become a passionate advocate of reform, an opponent of utility interests that were corrupting government on every level. He was dissatisfied with the world as he saw it and wanted to make it better; for his part, Mark Hanna was completely happy with a system that had returned him such bountiful millions, and opposed any tampering. Collision was inevitable.

Hanna and Johnson first locked horns in competition for a new franchise to extend their lines. Johnson got the franchise, and Hanna, who never could brook defeat, blamed Sims and demanded that Sims buy him out or sell. Sims sold and Hanna became the sole owner of the line.

The duel between Hanna and Johnson now waxed hotter than ever. A river divided Cleveland into two sections. Johnson's line ran on one side of the river, and he now sought a franchise to acquire a line on the other side, uniting the two and providing Clevelanders with one continuous ride across town for a nickel. This, to Hanna, was madness. Such a low fare, he thought, would be ruinous, and he fought it with all his fierce energy, hammering his cane on the floor of the city council chamber in his anger, buttonholing councilmen, endlessly pleading his cause.

Again he was defeated. Johnson won the bitter contest because Elias Sims controlled two votes in the city council. Sims hadn't forgiven Mark Hanna for his abrasive ways, and he got his revenge by providing the votes that gave Johnson his franchise. Hanna yowled that the cheap nickel fare would lead to bankruptcy, but it didn't. The unified new line turned out to be Johnson's most prosperous venture.

Johnson, like Mark Hanna later, now became more deeply involved in politics. He eventually sold out his streetcar interests to Hanna, who merged the two competing lines into one. Johnson then ran for mayor and was elected. Almost at once, he began to put into practice his theories about municipal ownership of utilities. He was convinced that streetcar lines could operate on a three-cent fare, and he forced the council to grant the necessary franchises to the city. This, to Hanna, was high treason. Red in the face with anger, he denounced Johnson as a radical, a Socialist, a wild man who would tear apart American society.

Determined to prevent such disaster, Hanna hurried off to the state capitol in Columbus and persuaded the attorney general to declare the city government of Cleveland unconstitutional. This incredible ruling was upheld by the courts, and soon all Ohio was in turmoil. For if the Cleveland government was unconstitutional, so was every other municipal government in the state. Faced with a chaotic collapse of all local administrations, the governor called a special session of the legislature to restore order.

The legislature straightened out the mess Hanna had created, but it turned down Hanna's pet project. This was a bill that would have given his own streetcar line a perpetual franchise. That was just too brazen a grab for even the corrupted, corporation-owned legislature to swallow; but Hanna had at least accomplished his main purpose. He had blocked the drive for municipal ownership.

The battle made him the hero of the iron, oil, gas, electric and manufacturing magnates—and their affiliated banks and real estate interests—who dominated the civic life of Cleveland. Hanna became their spokesman, a role that drew him ever more deeply into politics.

The Republican nominating convention of 1880 marked his emergence on the national scene. Hanna went to Chicago pledged to the Presidential aspirations of the veteran Ohioan, John Sherman, the Secretary of the Treasury. Hanna had a strong prejudice against Eastern money men and their smart operators. Sherman was a solid Westerner, a man who understood the needs of business—and hence, in Hanna's eyes, eminently suitable. To others, Sherman had serious drawbacks. He was crusty, proud, lacking in tact. He once called a Senator an ignoramous to his face and in public, which was not the way to make friends in politics. The convention would not have him and turned instead to a Civil War veteran, General James A. Garfield.

Eastern interests were disgruntled. Roscoe Conkling, the slippery and powerful New York boss, had attempted to spark a movement to draft Ulysses S. Grant, the victorious commander of the Union armies in the Civil War. Grant, after serving two terms in the White House, had just returned from a world tour and could be brought out of retirement for a third term. Conkling came to the convention with 306 votes pledged to Grant; but the West, much as it admired Grant, distrusted Conkling more. And so, after long balloting, the convention turned to a new face and picked Garfield.

Repudiated, Conkling threatened to shun the fall election campaign. But he was finally persuaded that he could not do this, so he agreed to make a token tour of Ohio. Collecting an entourage of dignitaries, he arranged to visit Grant's home in Warsaw. Mark Hanna, because he knew how to handle such things so well, was put in charge of transportation arrangements.

The rally at Warsaw was an enthusiastic one. Crowds turned out to gape at Grant and at all the important personages Conkling had brought with him from the East. Mark Hanna, mingling with the throng, began to be disturbed by an ugly rumor that was circulating. Conkling, so the story went, intended to take his party straight back to New York without paying a ritual visit to General Garfield's home in Mentor, Ohio. Such a snub would be politically damaging to Garfield, and Mark Hanna had no intention of letting it happen.

All the VIP's were at lunch when Hanna, who was not yet considered a VIP, pushed through the crowd into the dining room. He walked directly up to Grant and said: "General, it has been arranged that we return to Cleveland by way of Mentor, and if you propose to stop there and see General Garfield, we shall have to start in a very short time."

Conkling scowled, but he did not dare attempt to dictate to Grant. The general and former President looked into the bright brown eyes and determined face of the stocky man who confronted him, and he got the message.

"We will stop at Mentor," he said.

Mark Hanna had outmaneuvered Roscoe Conkling, the slickster from the East, and the rally at Mentor was a huge success, giving Garfield the invaluable blessing of Grant.

Back in Cleveland, working hard for the success of the Republican ticket, Hanna introduced a new wrinkle into national politics. He formed a Business Man's Republican Club, organizing Cleveland capitalists into an auxiliary political association to support the party that would benefit them most. Hanna whipped up enthusiasm by organizing and heading torchlight parades of businessmen, and the club raised sizeable sums for the Republican war chest. The idea caught on, and businessmen's Republican clubs were organized in many other cities.

Such services made Mark Hanna ever more powerful in Ohio politics. By 1884 he was recognized as one of Ohio's "big four," along with Sherman, McKinley, and Governor Joseph Benson Foraker. Foraker was an imposing man, tall, handsome and a fluent speaker. He had organized the Republican forces in southern, rural Ohio, and Hanna had helped to elect him by throwing behind him the weight of his growing machine. But the two men were made to distrust each other. Foraker was a bit too slick and too pompous for Hanna's taste, and Hanna was too direct, blunt and crude for Foraker's.

In 1884, however, they were still political allies. At the convention, Hanna stubbornly supported John Sherman; McKinley and Foraker backed James G. Blaine, of Maine, who was nominated. This difference of opinion did not split the political allies at that time; the break was to come four years later at the Republican convention of 1888.

Hanna, as usual, championed John Sherman, who was thought this time to have a good shot at the Presidential nomination. Foraker, who had Presidential aspirations himself, played a tricky game. In league with Blaine's Eastern followers, he was ready to start up a false boom for McKinley. The object was, not to nominate McKinley, but to split up John Sherman's home-state delegation, creating a deadlock that would lead to the renomination of Blaine, with Foraker the Vice Presidential candidate. However, McKinley scotched the plan. He had come to the convention pledged to Sherman, and he had no intention of betraying his candidate. When his name was called out by delegates from Connecticut, he rose and halted the roll-call of the states to make his intention plain; he would not run.

Foraker's crafty plan, which incensed Hanna, had been foiled. It was only one of many causes of discord between the two. Hanna, who had spent large sums of money supporting the governor, felt Foraker had reneged on a job promise made to one of his deserving political workers. Foraker, who had a very high opinion of himself, thought that Hanna, who had charge of convention arrangements for the Ohio delegation, had provided him with a hotel suite that did not do justice to his position. Added to this was Hanna's brazen, public purchase of the votes of poor Negro delegates from the South.

Foraker came upon Hanna in Sherman's headquarters, his hands full of currency, buying up the "tickets" that had been allotted to Southern delegates for gallery seats. Hanna, of course, didn't want the tickets; what he was buying were votes. Foraker, who could always strike the proper public attitude, pretended to be shocked to the bottom of his principled soul. Hanna, who was no hypocrite, bluntly defended his action. All candidates were buying votes, he said, accurately enough, and he was going to buy them for John Sherman where he could.

The result was the complete rupture of the Hanna-Foraker alliance and the beginning of a feud that was to rip apart the political landscape of Ohio for years to come. Even more important than the row with Foraker, however, was Mark Hanna's discovery of McKinley. McKinley's conduct in the 1888 convention had impressed Hanna. He admired a man who stood by his principles even in a hopeless cause as McKinley had in remaining steadfast to John Sherman, and Hanna was convinced from that moment that he had found the man whom one day he would make President. He knew now that John Sherman was getting too old to be nominated; and, as he told a friend, he "was going to stop riding the wrong horse."

William McKinley had all the political attributes. At the time of the 1888 convention, he was forty-five years old and had served six terms in Congress. He was a man who never made enemies if it could be helped, who never expressed controversial opinions, and one who, in the conduct of his domestic life, appeared so noble that lesser men accorded him their exaggerated admiration.

Tragedy had affected the mind of McKinley's wife, Ida. In 1873 she had had a hard time giving birth to her second daughter—and then the child had died. In 1876 her first daughter, Katie, also died; and the mother, mourning the loss of her children, became convinced that God was punishing her for some great, unnamed sin. She was never again quite right in the head; traces of epilepsy showed; and the word began to get around in Canton, Ohio, that Mrs. McKinley was subject to fits.

Another man might have been driven from his home to seek his pleasure elsewhere, but not William McKinley. A bouyant, gregarious man by nature, he changed into a soft-voiced, watchful nurse in his own home. His tender care of Ida, this warped and cantankerous woman, became the stuff of legend. Hanna, coming to know his true situation, exclaimed: "McKinley is a saint." Others attributed to him almost Christ-like qualities.

Such was the man whose cause Mark Hanna took up with all the energy and total commitment of his nature. Benjamin Harrison had won the Republican nomination in 1888, and big businessmen like Mark Hanna, eager to oust Grover Cleveland's Democrats from Washington, set out to buy themselves a national administration. Big business was committed to the erroneous proposition that no protective tariff could be too high and wanted an administration that would boost tariff rates almost out of sight. The purpose was frankly expressed in a fund-raising letter written by the president of the Republican League of the United States, a high-tariff lobby. He wrote: ". . . I would put the manufacturers of Pennsylvania under the fire and fry all the fat out of them."

This "frying the fat" technique raised huge campaign funds for

Harrison, who was elected by a wafer-thin margin over Cleveland. As a result, once in Washington, the new President found himself boxed in by ironclad pledges his campaign managers had made for him. "I could not name my own Cabinet," he said. "They had sold out every place to pay the election expenses."

With his party victorious, Mark Hanna rushed off to Washington to boost the political stock of his new protege. He wanted to make McKinley Speaker of the House of Representatives, but in this he failed. Thomas B. Reed had a larger following in the House and was chosen for the honor. Hanna had to settle for McKinley's appointment as chairman of the powerful House Ways and Means committee; and, by so doing, he almost ruined the future of the man he was determined to help.

McKinley was the perfect handmaiden—tool, if you will—of big business. It was not necessary to buy him; he believed, he was convinced. He set out to write a new and revolutionary tariff act. It was to be not just a protective tariff, but a *prohibitive* tariff. American industry was to be freed of all foreign competition. McKinley called in the special interests to be favored and told them to write their own rates. It was even too much for such a stout protectionist as Blaine, who tried to warn his party that it was courting disaster. But the big business lobby was firmly in control of Congress, and McKinley was its mouthpiece. He railed against competition by cheap European labor in terms like these: "Cheap is not a word of hope; it is not a word of inspiration! It is the badge of poverty; it is the signal of distress." And this at a time when the average American worker or farmer was earning $2 a day or less!

There was no echo of this harsh reality in McKinley's mellow voice when he rose in the House on May 7, 1890, to explain the wonders of the new tariff act his committee had concocted. It was, he said, an "American" act; it encouraged prosperity and the maintenance of the "American" standard (that $2 a day or less). "I believe in it," he said, his voice soaring, ". . . because enveloped in it are my country's highest development and greatest prosperity; out of it come the greatest gains to the people, the greatest comfort to the masses, the widest encouragement of manly aspirations, with the largest rewards, dignifying and elevating our citizenship, upon which the safety and purity and permanency of our political system depend."

This oratorical flight into the wild blue yonder led to a historic crash. Protected by the new "prohibitive" tariff, American business proceeded to gouge the consumer for everything he wore or ate. Fish cost a cent a pound more, cabbages three cents; duties were trebled on oranges and lemons—and so were their prices. Coal, blankets, carpets, tableware and kitchenware, women's and children's clothes —all suddenly cost more. The tinplate industry raised prices so outrageously that workingmen were gouged for everything from canned foods to tin buckets.

A Nebraskan later recalled for Thomas Beer what those days were like: ". . . I must try to convince you that our district was victimized by a kind of swindling that increased the hard times of 1891 and 1892. The railroad overcharged for everything. You know that it was cheaper to burn corn for fuel in 1888 and 1889 than to ship it. We were absolutely at the mercy of the railroads and the express companies. . . .

"Another form of swindling was that used by some storekeepers in such small communities. I know that a lot of sentimentalism has been expended on the dear old whimsical fellow who has a general store by some of our writers of rural hokum. But the storekeeper was frequently a hard-fisted cheat. In 1890, when the McKinley tariff bill passed Congress, this smart Heinie in our town put up all prices 'on aggount of the dariff.' It was then that our banker came to the rescue. He told this robber baron to put the prices down or he would open an opposition store. Of course the storekeeper dropped his prices instanter. . . ."

Such public-spirited bankers were exceptions to the rule; and in the nation as a whole, there were no forces to alleviate the effects of the McKinley tariff. Instead of the promised prosperity, it brought depression and disaster. A new grass-roots political movement—the People's Party, whose followers became known as Populists—sprang up through the farming Midwest, preaching a creed of hatred for the Eastern moguls who had been the architects of such hard times. A roar of outrage and protest swept the nation. When McKinley ran for re-election in November, 1890, Democrats sent peddlers all through his district to dramatize the tariff issue. They offered tin cups worth five cents for twenty-five cents and "cheap" coffeepots for $1.50. The effect was devastating.

McKinley, who had been elected so many times he was considered virtually unbeatable in his district, went down to defeat. He was by no means alone. His tariff act had produced a national repudiation of his party. Such traditional Republican strongholds as Ohio, Michigan, Illinois, Wisconsin, Kansas, and Massachusetts sent Democrats to Congress; and when the House of Representatives organized for the new session in 1891, the Republicans had been swept out like victims floundering in a tidal wave. The Democrats held 235 seats, the Populists nine; the Republicans only eighty-eight, their smallest bloc since the Civil War.

Mark Hanna was appalled by this unanticipated hurricane of public reaction; but naturally, being the man he was, it did not shake his faith in the holiness of his cause. William McKinley had been booted out of Congress by an ungrateful electorate? Then there was only one thing to do: make him governor of Ohio.

Mark Hanna, with his persistence that would never admit defeat, set out immediately to do just this—to turn the defeat of 1890 into the triumph of 1891. There can be no question about the methods that he used. A blunt man, he spoke so openly about his philosophy and his methods that he shocked many who agreed privately with him. The state to Mark Hanna had to be "a business state." A group of business companions almost choked on their food at dinner on one occasion when he declared for all to hear that "all questions of government in a democracy were questions of money."

Acting on this principle, Hanna now pressured local capitalists to raise a slush fund to make William McKinley governor. He did not stop with the fat cats of Ohio, but made forays into neighboring Indiana and Illinois. Here his pitch was that big business could not afford to let the Republicans lose Ohio, nor could it afford to lose William McKinley, the best friend big business ever had. Enormous sums were raised and wisely spent. So McKinley got the Republican nomination for governor; and in the fall election of 1891, while Democrats were again sweeping the country, the combination of McKinley's "sainthood" and Mark Hanna's money triumphed in Ohio. The victory made McKinley a national political property, a politician who had accomplished the feat politicians most respect by swimming successfully upstream against a hostile tide.

There remained only for Mark Hanna to finish off Joseph Foraker—and this he now did. Foraker wanted to oust the veteran John Sherman from the U.S. Senate. Senators were selected in those days, not by popular vote, but by the state legislatures. Hanna threw himself and his millionaire's bankroll into the battle to make certain that the shifty Foraker did not replace Sherman. Money flowed as freely as whiskey during the showdown in the state capitol at Columbus. Hanna's hard-driven agents hunted down legislators in remote districts all over the state, and in one way or another "persuaded" them to vote for John Sherman. In the final roll-call, Foraker was soundly defeated. Mark Hanna once again had demonstrated his political power; he was now, in effect, the uncrowned king of Ohio.

A member of the Ohio legislature later declared that, from this moment on, the law firm employed by Mark Hanna in Cleveland dominated the actions of the state legislature. He said: "No bill was permitted to come out of committee until Mr. Hanna's lawyers had first examined and approved it. . . . Money was rarely used. It was not necessary. . . . But . . . there was something behind the lobby that worked with clocklike precision and extended over the entire state. It included the local press and press agencies, the Chambers of Commerce and the county rings. . . . Ohio, in short . . . was ruled by business. Not by all business, but by bankers, steam-railroads, public-utility corporations. . . ."

Thus Hanna had laid a firm foundation for the Presidential drive of William McKinley; but he knew as the 1892 campaign approached that the time was not yet. President Harrison would certainly be renominated by his party; and, besides, the bad times that had descended upon the country after the passage of the McKinley tariff in 1890 had persisted and deepened into a full-fledged depression. The thing to do, as Hanna recognized, was to build up his man for the campaign of 1896; and this meant re-electing McKinley governor of Ohio by a landslide vote in the state election of 1893.

It was at this point that a private financial disaster of McKinley's almost wrecked Hanna's plans. As a young man, McKinley had borrowed $5,000 from a Youngstown tin-can manufacturer to finance his way through law school. He had never bothered to repay the loan. Later, when McKinley was governor, his early benefactor asked him to sign some notes. McKinley obliged, making himself responsible for some $130,000 worth of the man's borrowings if his business should fail. The depression had now wrecked this tin-can manufacturer's business—and McKinley was caught.

He could not possibly pay such a sum. He was, in effect, bankrupt and now considered abandoning his political career and returning to the practice of law so that he could gradually pay off his creditors. Yet Mark Hanna would not hear of it. He took charge of the ruined governor's finances and formed a "syndicate" whose sole purpose was to pay off the $130,000 and keep alive the valuable political property represented in William McKinley.

Under the spur of Hanna, big business magnates in many fields —ironmasters, steel and machinery manufacturers, bankers and railroad owners—charged to the rescue with their wallets open. Soon McKinley's debt was liquidated, and he was re-elected governor in 1893. He was never told, so it was said, the identity of the wealthy Good Samaritans who had rescued him from such dire financial trouble; and it was, of course, just sheer coincidence that many of these unidentified benefactors were soon to be rewarded with Cabinet posts and prestigious ambassadorships abroad.

Hanna decided that the time had now come to abandon business for politics. At the end of 1894, he startled his business associates by turning over the active direction of the affairs of M. A. Hanna & Co. to his brother Leonard and devoting all of his energies to the task of making William McKinley President.

A cartoon in the *Cleveland Leader* had caught Hanna's eye. It showed McKinley's beaming countenance rising like the sun over a land wracked by depression, strikes, and violence, and Uncle Sam pointing to these happy features as the Rising Sun of Prosperity. Hanna seized upon the idea and soon billboards and posters were plastered across the land, hailing McKinley as "The Advance Agent of Prosperity." It was only the first step in Hanna's ambitious campaign to "package" William McKinley the way a businessman would a breakfast cereal and sell him to the American people.

A second major project involved the wrapping up of delegate votes from the South before rivals knew what was happening. Early in 1895, Hanna set aside a sum usually estimated at $100,000 and bought a winter home in Thomasville, Georgia. He let it be known that he was simply trying to escape the rigors of the harsh Ohio winter; and it was, of course, only natural that his good friend, Governor William McKinley, should visit him from time to time to get the benefits of the Southern sunshine. If Hanna also entertained key Southern politicians when McKinley was present—well, that was only natural, wasn't it?

McKinley, amiable, kindly, always saying the right thing at the right time, made pat little speeches to such gatherings, and many of the callers went away impressed. Without doubt, McKinley presented the perfect Presidential façade with his broad, noble brow and his firm steady eye. But William Allen White, one of the most famous journalists of the day, found little substance behind the mask. He wrote that McKinley had "a face without vision but without guile," that he was "on the whole decent, on the whole dumb," and that he rarely reached "above the least common denominator of the popular intelligence." Acidly, White added: "He walked among men like a bronze statue . . . determinedly looking for his pedestal."

Mark Hanna, of course, did not rely alone on the impression his "bronze statue" might make. For Hanna's pocketbook was open, and his money was working on a more pragmatic political level. State chairmen and the secretaries of state Republican committees were all lured into what Hanna called his "combinations"; and with such powers in his pocket, he made certain that the delegates chosen to attend the national convention were all "the right kind of men"—men who would vote for William McKinley. By such methods, he rounded up a bloc of nearly 200 solid Southern delegates. Tom Platt, who had become the boss of the New York State Republican machine, later commented admiringly: "Hanna . . . had the South practically solid before some of us awakened."

Having stolen this march on the opposition, Hanna next raided the Western and Pacific slope states. Then he switched his tactics and made a daring foray into the East, capturing the votes of Vermont with the aid of some powerful big business interests there. All of these delegate votes, added to McKinley's base strength in Ohio and neighboring Midwestern states, virtually assured the nomination before the Republican National Convention even convened in St. Louis in mid-June, 1896.

There remained only one important issue, the candidate's stand on the coinage of free silver. The depression of the 1890s—and the Panic of 1893—had led to a great outcry through the West for more and easier money. Huge silver mines had been discovered, and the demand for more money—in the hope that, if there were more, it might find its way into the pockets of the farmers and the poor—focused on giving silver a standard comparable to gold. American currency at the time, like the currencies of all foreign countries, was based upon the so-called gold standard (that is, paper money could be redeemed in gold); and Eastern bankers and financiers were appalled at what might happen if the West had its way and money suddenly became "cheap."

McKinley as a Congressman had tended to side with the free-silver bloc, and Hanna realized that this was an issue that would have to be handled as gingerly as a high-wire walker performing in the circus. McKinley must side with the big-money (gold) interests of the East, but he must do so in a fashion that would not lose him the West—that, indeed, would leave the West still believing he was a free-silver man at heart.

Such trickery required that the candidate should keep his mouth shut—not too difficult a feat for McKinley where a vital issue was concerned. The press, the politicians, everyone it seemed, all were clamoring to know where Hanna and McKinley stood on the burning issue of free silver. There were no answers, and the clamor grew. Hanna let it grow; indeed, he wanted it to grow. He wanted to be placed in a position in which it would appear, when he made his move, that his candidate's reluctant hand had been forced, but his heart was still in the right place.

The Eastern money interests, led by J. P. Morgan, became ever more frantic, and they served a virtual ultimatum. The party platform must declare emphatically for the gold standard. And soon a young politician who bore one of the most famous names in Massachusetts, Senator Henry Cabot Lodge, confronted a burly, perspiring, overworked Hanna with this demand:

"You'll put this in the platform or we'll rip you up the back!" Lodge threatened.

"Who in hell are you?" Hanna demanded.

"Senator Henry Cabot Lodge, of Massachusetts."

"Well, Senator Henry Cabot Lodge, of Massachusetts, you can go plumb to hell. You have nothing to say about it."

This rough handling of the great man from the East was marvelous window-dressing for the predetermined move that might distress the West. In the end, having reaped all the political advantage that they could from their farcical play-acting, Hanna and McKinley backed the perfect straddle. The platform plank they finally approved declared they were "unreservedly for sound money" and opposed "the free coinage of silver" except by international agreement. McKinley pledged that he would work for such an agreement. It was a meaningless promise. The Eastern bankers had had their way, and a sop had been thrown to the West to keep it from revolt.

With McKinley nominated, Hanna had planned to relax with a vacation cruise along the New England coast; but the Democrats, meeting in Chicago in July, upset all his plans. A new—and to Hanna, a menacing—figure stormed upon the public scene. He was William Jennings Bryan, the so-called "Boy Orator of the Platte."

Indeed, Bryan was one of the greatest orators American politics has ever produced. He led a grass-roots revolt against Eastern financial interests that had dominated the Democratic Party just as they had the Republican; and in a speech whose eloquence stampeded the convention, he captured the Democratic Presidential nomination.

Some of Bryan's phrases, even in cold print today, still ring with the eloquence with which he invested them; some drew issues that were to divide the two major parties far beyond his own time. For example:

"There are those who believe that, if you will only legislate to make the well-to-do prosperous, their prosperity will leak through to those below. The Democratic idea, however, has been that if you will legislate to make the masses prosperous, their prosperity will find its way up through every class which rests upon them."

Capitalizing on the miseries of the time, he drew the lines of class distinction—the workers and the farmers against the monied classes that had captured control of the government and had legislated in their own self-interest.

Bryan's magnificent voice soared as he thundered:

"We have petitioned, and our petitions have been scorned; we have entreated, and our entreaties have been disregarded; we have begged, and they have mocked when our calamity came. We beg no longer; we entreat no more; we petition no more. [A dramatic pause.] *We defy them.*"

Those last words brought a thunderous roar from 20,000 throats. But Bryan was not yet done. He had saved his best lines for the last. In a flaming final burst of oratory, he set the convention wild and uttered the phrases that would make him famous:

". . . Having behind us the producing masses of this nation and the world, supported by the commercial interests, the laboring interests, and the toilers everywhere, we will answer their demand for a gold standard by saying to them: *You shall not press down upon the brow of labor this crown of thorns, you shall not crucify mankind upon a cross of gold."*

This "Cross of Gold" speech, as it came to be known forever after, touched off one of the most hectic Presidential campaigns in American history. The tireless Bryan stormed up and down the nation, traveling 18,000 miles and making more than 600 speeches in three months. He drew enormous crowds, addressing in person more than five million listeners. He posed a threat to Mark Hanna and the millionaires he represented. To them, Bryan was a wild man, a radical; he must be stopped at all costs.

Hanna threw himself into the task of building the roadblock. He descended upon New York like some elemental whirlwind from the west. Finding many capitalists in a state of funk, he lashed out at them scornfully at a dinner in the Union League Club. "There won't be a revolution. You are damned fools," he told them scornfully.

Hanna was indomitable and canny. His courage bucked them up; and at the same time, seeing how fearful they were, he took advantage of their fears. He embarked upon a "frying the fat" campaign unprecedented in American political history up to that time. No one will ever know precisely how much money he shook out of the fat cats, but the sum was colossal. One or two million dollars had been considered sufficient to run a national campaign before this time; but Hanna set his goal at $10 million to $15 million. And all the indications are that, before the campaign was over, he got this amount— and more.

Under his guidance, McKinley ran a campaign that was the very opposite of Bryan's. It became known as "the front porch campaign," and it was designed to build the image of a calm, reasonable, statesmanlike McKinley—a man in sharp contrast with his frantic, ranting rival.

Nothing was left to chance. McKinley simply stayed at his home in Canton, Ohio, and received delegations of visitors who represented influential groups in the electorate. These delegations were carefully screened and organized by Hanna and his aides until they were, in the end, like so many trained seals. Their expenses were paid for their much-publicized pilgrimages to Canton; they were briefed on the questions they were permitted to ask the candidate; and McKinley's answers to the planted questions were carefully written out in advance to avoid any chance of a damaging slipup.

The candidate, donning his most saintly air, mouthed empty phrases about the "dignity of labor" and harped on the dire consequences to the average workingman if a "cheap dollar" whittled away his buying power. He figuratively raised his hands in horror at Bryan's appeal to class prejudice; ours, he said again and again, was a "classless" society, with "all equal citizens and equal in privilege and opportunity"—a pronouncement that ignored the reality of class divisions in which business had, in effect, captured the control of the government and legislated in its own self-interest.

While McKinley was performing this charade in Canton, Mark Hanna hurried back to New York on August 15 in another money-raising raid on the resources of big business. He was joined by James J. Hill, the railroad tycoon from St. Paul, Minnesota; and day after day the two rode in their carriage to the offices of the mighty in Wall Street. Again Hanna left nothing to chance. He did not ask or beg for money; he assessed. He demanded one-quarter of one percent of the capital assets of every business—and he got it.

Standard Oil contributed $250,000; J. P. Morgan matched the amount; the four great packing houses of Chicago kicked in a reported $400,000. Insurance companies turned over large parts of their clients' premiums—a deed comparable to a bank's giving up part of its depositors' money—to aid the Republican campaign.

Having raised enormous boodle, Hanna went back to the West, determined to beat Bryan in the Populist sections where his appeal was most dangerous. He flooded the nation with some 120 million copies of 275 different pamphlets, written in a variety of languages, to explain Republican views on the money issue. Below the high road there was a low road, one of the ugliest in American history.

With panic spreading that Bryan might sweep the country with his great popular appeal, businesses of every stripe began a campaign of outright intimidation of their workers. Vote for Byran, workers were told, and there won't be any jobs for you the day after election. Workers who were active Democrats were threatened with dismissal. On the Saturday before election, with the issue in Chicago still in the balance, railroad leaders and powerful manufacturers issued a final ultimatum to their work forces: if Bryan were elected on Tuesday, none need to report for work on Wednesday. Or, as the head of the Steinway piano works was reported to have said, "the whistle will not blow on Wednesday morning."

Democrats held a last-minute conference, hoping to find a way to make such tactics backfire, but one of their veteran leaders shook his head and said perceptively: "Boys, I'm afraid this beats us. If I were a working man and had nothing but my job, I am afraid when I came to vote I would think of Mollie and the babies."

He was right—and yet, perhaps, not wholly right. Even with such pressures, McKinley might not have won had not Hanna padded the ballot boxes of the nation on a scale that would have awed even Boss Tweed. The enormous Hanna campaign kitty bankrolled an army of election workers who imported Negroes by the trainload across the Mason-Dixon line from the South. At many points, it was reported, "the very graveyards were robbed of the names on their tombstones." One Western district having only 30,000 registered voters counted 48,000 votes. Some 30,000 floaters poured into Indiana; and in Ohio, an incredible one out of every four living persons (with women and children not eligible to vote) were counted as having cast their ballots.

Inevitably, McKinley won. Bryan polled 6.5 million votes, more than had ever been cast before for a Presidential candidate, but McKinley tallied 7 million. The vote in the electoral college was decisive, with Republicans carrying states having 271 electoral votes to the Democrats' 176. But, as later analyses showed, a shift of just 14,000 votes in six states—California, Oregon, Kentucky, Indiana, North Dakota, and West Virginia (some of them carried by only a few hundred votes)—would have changed the entire result and given Bryan a clear-cut victory. It had not happened because Mark Hanna, in his ruthless way, had pulled out every trick in the political carpet-bag to bulldoze his way to victory. "God's in his Heaven, all's right with the world!" he exulted in a telegram to McKinley.

His joy was a bit premature, but essentially he was right. Hanna and the Republicans had no more idea than the Democrats how to solve the long-lasting economic ills that had beset the country ever since the post-Civil War boom had burst. But events over which they had no control came to their aid and made it seem to the average man that the GOP was, as Hanna proclaimed, the party of "the full dinner pail."

Just before the election of 1896, the Indian wheat crop had failed. This created a huge export market for American surplus wheat, prices soared, and the farm states suddenly became prosperous. Shortly afterwards, early in the new administration, a disastrous drought ruined the French wheat crop, and the Russian crop was damaged by storms and rain. Millions upon millions of bushels of wheat were shipped overseas; payment in gold flowed back; and the price of wheat went to $1 a bushel on the Chicago market.

In addition to all this, great new gold mines were discovered and opened up in the West, and improved extraction processes increased the yield from old mines. Suddenly, there was an abundance of wealth as gold reserves which had been $44 million in 1896 mushroomed to $245 million in 1898. A new construction and industrial boom, with old plants modernized and new ones constructed, swept the country, bringing with it jobs and prosperity.

The McKinley Administration reveled in its good fortune, and Hanna, the man who single-handedly had created it, was determined to be a part of it. President McKinley lifted John Sherman out of the Senate and made him Secretary of State. This left Ohio with only one U.S. Senator, and, of course, Mark Hanna was appointed to the vacant post.

The appointment was good only until the next election; and Hanna, at the age of 60, had to take to the stump. He proved a good, rough-and-tumble campaign orator as he strove to get enough Republicans elected to the Ohio legislature to insure his own victory. The trouble was that there were independents in his own party, and these united with the Democrats to try to block the selection of Hanna.

A riotous scene resulted in Columbus. One Hanna supporter was kidnaped and held prisoner by the opposition; Hanna's forces recaptured him, spirited him back into their own camp, and locked him up. When the voting started, a free-silver Republican, J. C. Otis, hurled a bombshell. He declared he had been offered a $1,750 bribe to vote for Hanna—and he produced the $1,750. Even this sensational development could not stop the Hanna steamroller as the majority of Ohio legislators, under his control, voted to send him back to Washington.

Demands were made for an investigation that would oust Hanna from his Senate seat. Hardly anyone, not even his own supporters, doubted the veracity of Otis's charge; but Hanna's party was in control of the legislative machinery in Washington, and the whole issue was quietly buried.

Mark Hanna as a U.S. Senator was a force that was felt rather than seen or heard. He was not a polished speaker, and being a man who was honest with himself, he recognized his limitations and spoke rarely. But everyone in Washington recognized his hidden power. Office seekers swarmed about his office and his home; his mail was heavier than any official's except the President, and he had to hire a secretariat to handle it. When the clamor of those wanting a job or a favor or aid to pass a pending bill became just too overwhelming, he sometimes sought refuge in his dentist's chair.

The election campaign of 1900, unlike that of 1896, was an almost cut-and-dried affair. There was no question about the candidates; McKinley and Bryan would again face each other. There was not even much question about the outcome; with the country prosperous, with the brief Spanish-American War having been won, McKinley rode a tide of popularity unmatched by any American President since Lincoln. There was only one question: Who would be McKinley's Vice Presidential running mate?

Mark Hanna was still chairman of the Republican National Committee, still the national boss of his party. But he had a rebellion on his hands. In New York, Boss Tom Platt wanted to get rid of a thorn in his side. The thorn was bumptious, dynamic Theodore Roosevelt, a man no political boss could control. And so Platt, lobbying with his boss counterparts in the Eastern states, came up with a marvelous solution: They would "bury" Teddy Roosevelt forever by stashing him away in the Vice Presidency, where he would have no power and could be forgotten.

Hanna was opposed to the scheme. "Don't you understand," he asked angrily, "that there is just one life between this crazy man and the Presidency if you force me to take Roosevelt?"

For once, he was overborne. The combination of the party bosses was too strong, and Hanna yielded. Theodore Roosevelt became William McKinley's Vice President.

Then the tragedy that Mark Hanna had foreseen as a possibility happened. On September 6, 1901, as McKinley was shaking hands with well-wishers at the Pan American Exposition in Buffalo, New York, a nondescript anarchist named Leon Czolgosz, a pistol hidden in a handkerchief, shot McKinley in the stomach as the President reached out to shake his hand. Eight days later, after an infection set in McKinley died, and "that madman," as Hanna had sometimes called Roosevelt, was in the White House.

Even so, even though Roosevelt in many ways fought the entrenched economic powers that Hanna represented, the stubborn old Senator from Ohio remained a force to be reckoned with. The new President found it wise to consult him on almost every issue. So powerful was Hanna that his mail continued to be larger in volume than that of all other Senators put together; so powerful was he that, if he wished to talk to a Cabinet officer he sent for him, if he wished to consult in private with constituents, he simply appropriated the office of the Vice President.

Moreover, Hanna was still the idol of Wall Street, of big business, of all the forces that hated Roosevelt. There was much talk that he should oppose Roosevelt for the Republican Presidential nomination in 1904; but Mark Hanna, wiser than many of his supporters, drew back from making the challenge. He recognized Roosevelt's enormous popularity with the masses, and he had no taste for a campaign that he felt could end only in defeat. And so, instead, he ran for re-election as Senator from Ohio.

It was a gruelling campaign, but Mark Hanna won as he had almost always won. It was his last victory. The human machine that he had driven so hard in his fierce contests was wearing out. He became ill, rallied, failed again. Then he contracted typhoid fever, and on February 15, 1904, he died in his rooms in the Arlington Hotel in Washington.

He had been, for all practical purposes, a national political boss, the first and only one of his kind—the man who made a President. He had also changed the political balance of the country in a fundamental way. Big business did not just buy political influence as it always had; millionaires now seated themselves in political chairs, comprising at times almost the entirety of the Cabinets in Republican administrations. And the nation, as a whole, approved, so completely had Mark Hanna imbedded in the public mind the idea that the Republican Party was the party of prosperity and "the full dinner pail" for every workingman. It was a belief, a faith, that was to last far beyond his own time until the worst depression in the nation's history, erupting in 1929 in the midst of the Hoover regime that so faithfully reflected Republican philosophy, finally exposed the fallacy of the idea of businessmen's omniscience in the affairs of government.

5

Abe Ruef,
Labor Boss

ABRAHAM RUEF BECAME a political boss by championing the interests of labor, just as Mark Hanna had risen to prominence as the
power broker of big business. But there all similarity ended. Ruef,
who aspired to national power just as Hanna had, fathered one of the
most corrupt regimes of his time and saw his ambitions crash in an
exposé unrivaled for sensationalism.

It happened in San Francisco at the turn of the century. This
city, set on its high hills above its sparkling bay looking westward to
the Golden Gate, is sometimes called the most beautiful in America,
but in the early 1900s it was only a few steps removed from the
brawling frontier town that it had been. For decades after the gold
rush of 1849, San Francisco remained a city of harlots, gamblers,
thugs, and opportunists of every stripe. It was a city rampant with
crime and violence, a situation that led in turn to vigilantes—
volunteers who took the law into their own hands, punishing and
lynching in the cause of law and order.

Such was the atmosphere of the city in which Abe Ruef grew to
manhood and aspired to power. He became the architect of a labor
regime that finally seized complete control of the city government.
Just as this was a unique development—labor never wields such total
authority in America—so was Reuf himself a distinctive and highly
unusual type of political boss.

Most of America's political bosses have not been especially well-educated or intellectual. The system ordinarily spawns the type of scrappers who come up through the muck of ward politics. They are gifted with a native cunning, a lack of scruples, and the requisite ruthlessness, a combination that eliminates less astute or less hardened competitors. Abe Ruef was the very opposite of such men.

He was born in San Francisco on September 2, 1864. His father had operated a dry goods store and prospered in real estate; he was known in the city as a "capitalist." Young Ruef was so intellectually brilliant that he graduated from the University of California at the age of eighteen. He spoke several languages and was fascinated with philosophy, art, and music—interests utterly foreign to most political bosses.

Standing five feet eight, Ruef was a handsome young man, with dark curly hair and a dark mustache. He had the kind of quick wit that later enabled him to confront politicial hecklers and turn the tables on them. He had tremendous energy and, unfortunately, the kind of limitless ambition that led him to seek the golden end without troubling his conscience about the means.

Admitted to the bar in 1886, Abe Ruef, with his exceptional talents, should have had a prosperous and legitimate career before him. But with his energy and ambition he coveted power. He began as a political reformer, founding the Municipal Reform League and corresponding for a time with other young rebels like Theodore Roosevelt in New York. But it soon became obvious to Ruef that a reform party would never rise above the ruck that buries such splinter efforts in American politics. The route to prominence and power lay through the established parties.

And so, in 1886, the same year in which he became a lawyer, Ruef began to dabble in Republican politics. His first step was to attend what was supposed to be the rally of a district club. The site was in one of the most disreputable parts of the city, and when Ruef arrived, he found just two men present. They told him he had come just too late; there had been a large and enthusiastic rally, but the crowd had dispersed. Ruef was about to leave when one asked him: "Young man, can you write?" Ruef acknowledged that he possessed this rare skill, and so he was named on the spot the secretary of the Republican club. His two mentors described for him the rally that had just been held, Ruef wrote up a glowing account, took it to the newspapers, and saw it published the next day. Only later did he learn that there never had been a rally; those who might have come had been afraid to venture into such a lawless district, and the two men he had met were, in effect, "the club."

It was a fitting introduction into a world of politics marked by violence and fraud. Pitched battles were often fought on election day between rival gangs known as "rockrollers." Ballot boxes were stuffed, and the results tallied in secret. Money was used freely to buy votes, finance corrupt newspapers, and pay for the small armies of political mercenaries known as "the push." Behind all this were the most powerful interests in California. The Southern Pacific Railroad, allied with other utilities and big businesses, bought up politicians wholesale and literally ran the state. It was often said that the capital of California was not in Sacramento, but in the San Francisco law office of William F. Herrin, the political agent of Southern Pacific.

Into this political cesspool stepped the ambitious Abe Ruef. Later, in an attempt to justify himself, he described how the dying Republican boss, Bill Higgins, summoned him and asked him to support his principal lieutenants, Phil Crimmins and Martin Kelly. Ruef lent class to the party, Higgins felt. When Ruef went to see Kelly in the back room of Crimmins' saloon, he found a judge hob-nobbing at the bar with some of the political hangers-on. It was an encounter of deep significance. Ruef could see that a lawyer who, as a politician, helped to make a man a judge would have more than ordinary influence with His Honor. The temptation was too great. Ruef involved himself ever more deeply in the seamy side of ward politics; and, as his political power grew, so in proportion did his law business.

Yet he still fluctuated back and forth at times between the soiled mechanics of the regular machine and the idealism of the reformers. But he found "the people were apathetic," and he cast aside "whatever ideals I once had." He devoted himself to the machine brand of politics and became known in time as "the boss of the Latin Quarter."

Actually, this later self-justification of Ruef's conflicts with the facts. The people of San Francisco were by no means so apathetic as Ruef pictured them, for it was just at this time, during the period from 1892 to 1900, that the city was undergoing a species of reform. James D. Phelan, son of a San Francisco capitalist and himself a millionaire, ran for mayor in 1896 at the head of a Democratic reform ticket. He was elected and re-elected, holding office for the next five years. Personally incorruptible, Phelan gave the city one of the best administrations it had ever had; and in 1900 he secured the passage of a new charter, giving the office of mayor, which had previously been something of a figurehead position, sweeping new powers. The record would seem to indicate not the hopelessness of reform, not apathy, but the misplacement of Ruef's own loyalties, for Ruef was on the side of the crooks.

The years of Phelan-Democratic-reform dominance had been lean ones for bosses like Crimmins and Kelly, but they still kept their grip on the local Republican organization. Ruef looked upon them with contempt, not so much because of their methods but their failures; he believed he could do better. In the primary election of 1900, he rebelled and tried to seize control of the local Republican organization with an insurgent slate, but the Crimmins-Kelly machine steamrollered its way right over him. Ruef had failed in his first bid for power. Almost immediately, events conspired to give him a new and better chance.

San Francisco was a strong union town. Patrick Henry McCarthy, who had come to the city in 1886, the same year Ruef began to practice law, had formed the Building Trades Council of San Francisco and had made it virtually all-powerful in the construction industry. The city was remote enough so that it was not easy to bring in strike-breakers, and many employers found it to their advantage to yield to McCarthy's demands and pass the higher costs along to the public. Bricklayers were given quotas of the number of bricks they could lay in a day; the size of paint brushes was limited so that painters would not finish a job too quickly; plumbers took only their own sons into their union; and there were years when no apprentices were trained in the building trades. This kept the labor market tight, wages up; and the employer-union collusion gave San Francisco's workingmen far higher incomes than were being earned elsewhere. It was a situation that could not last forever.

In 1901, the employers became restive. They formed the Employers Association to fight the San Francisco Labor Council, which represented workers less fortunate than those in McCarthy's building trades unions. A showdown came in July when the employers decided to break the new Teamsters' Union. When they refused to meet the teamsters' demands, a strike followed. It became known as the San Francisco general strike, a misnomer because the strike was not general. It involved mainly the waterfront; and by the end of July some 15,000 teamsters, dock workers, sailors, and warehousemen were on strike. The effect was to tie up the port and make the shipment overseas of farm produce and other products impossible.

Mayor Phelan, who had fought the long and good fight against corruption, was the man in the middle. Phelan had abolished the standard practice of bribing the Board of Supervisors, the city's legislative body. He had pared contracts. He had discovered that the gas company was charging the city an exorbitant rate for street gas lights and that it had installed more lights than were needed. He had also eliminated 600 lights at one stroke—a deed that caused him to be immediately ostracized by the fashionable Pacific Union Club, whose members could not tolerate a man who would do such a thing to business. But now business was really hurting, the whole city was hurting; and pressure mounted on Phelan to break the strike.

The Employers Association got non-union men to handle the wagons idled by the striking teamsters and demanded police protection for them. A businessman himself, Phelan sympathized with his own business class in this crisis; and, in the end, after some hesitation, he yielded. He put policemen on the wagons, with orders to see that they were kept moving through the streets. Violence swiftly followed. Angry mobs of strikers attacked the wagons and their police guards. On September 29, 1901, there was a bloody riot. Police clubbed and beat the strikers; men were crippled and killed. Three days later, the strike ended in a compromise settlement that was generally interpreted as a victory for the employers.

The unions were bitter. They felt that the law had not been impartial, but had been used savagely against them. To prevent this happening again, they thought, they would have to go into politics and try to get control of the city government. The result was the formation of the Union Labor Party.

Ruef, who had failed in his bid to take over the Republican machine, became intrigued. With labor in its bitter mood, with his own personal following which he might be able to switch from its normal Republican allegiance, he saw an opportunity to capture the mayoralty in a three-party fight. Furthermore, he really became excited when he heard a rumor that the new labor party was considering running Eugene E. Schmitz, president of the musicians' union, for mayor.

Schmitz and Ruef, both thirty-seven at the time, had been

friends for fifteen years, and Ruef was Schmitz's attorney. Schmitz was an accomplished violinist and had won some local fame as a composer. What was more important, he made an imposing impression. Fremont Older, managing editor of the San Francisco *Bulletin*, the man who was to be the nemesis of both Schmitz and Ruef, later wrote of Schmitz: "He was every inch the right looking man for a candidate. Tall, well-formed, handsome, always well-dressed and self-possessed, he was a commanding figure of a man, the center of all eyes in a crowd." He had also, as Ruef wrote, "a tenacious memory and an unsurpassable nerve."

Schmitz laughed at first at the idea that he should run for mayor. He had never made a political speech in his life; he knew nothing of politics, he said. Ruef told him not to worry; he would take care of everything. He would write the speeches; all Schmitz had to do was deliver them. Finally, Schmitz agreed, and Ruef quietly packed the Union Labor Party convention with his own men. He captured control of the new party, wrote a moderate platform deliberately designed not to create undue alarm, and composed a five-minute speech for Schmitz. A skillful actor, Schmitz delivered the speech as if it were his own and as if he were speaking off the cuff; he brought down the house and was nominated on the spot.

The general election campaign developed much the way Ruef had envisioned it. The Republican and Democratic parties had their own candidates. Labor, except for McCarthy's Building Trades Council, united solidly behind Schmitz. Ruef, the ever-active gremlin behind the scenes, even wooed some secret business support. The fact that he himself was an attorney and a large real estate operator helped to allay businessmen's fears, and there were some cynical enough to think it would be great sport to elect a labor mayor whom business could secretly control through Ruef.

Out front, of course, was Schmitz. The man was a revelation. Ruef wrote the speeches, and Schmitz delivered them with fire and fervor, as if they came straight from his heart. With his handsome, commanding presence and his innate gift of oratory, he quickly established himself as the most colorful campaign personality San Francisco had seen in a long time.

This kind of vigorous, all-out campaign naturally required money. Funds had to be spent for placards, banners, meeting halls, bands, and parades—all the hoopla that marked heated campaigns in those days. Ruef claimed that he spent $16,000 of his own money on the campaign. As he later wrote, in words that are perhaps even more true today than they were then: "Elections cannot be carried without money, and large amounts of money at that. . . . Somebody with an interest must put it up. The interest may not always be corrupt, but it is always selfish."

When the votes were counted, Schmitz was elected, polling 4,000 votes more than his nearest competitor in the three-way race. The Union Labor Party, however, elected only three of the eighteen-man Board of Supervisors, and so, though it had captured the mayor's office, it did not yet have complete control of the municipal government.

With this first victory, Ruef's ambitions soared. He spirited Schmitz away to a Sonoma hideaway where he gave the new mayor an intensive cram course in the mysteries of municipal government. While educating the new mayor, Ruef let his imagination picture a beautiful vista of the future. He envisioned the Union Labor Party expanding beyond the city to all of California, even to other states. Indeed, he saw himself as the architect of a new political movement that would elevate Schmitz to the Presidency and put himself in the U.S. Senate, a labor-political script that paralleled in almost every detail the king-making methods of Mark Hanna on behalf of big business.

Although Ruef did not realize it at the time, he was heading for the confrontation of his life. His role in masterminding the election of Schmitz had not escaped the notice of one of the most remarkable men in San Francisco—the editor Fremont Older. Older was a big, tall, strong-willed and sometimes passionately emotional man. He had supported Phelan; he loathed graft; and he wanted for the city the same kind of clean administration he felt Phelan had given it.

When it came to graft, Older had an embarrassingly direct, personal knowledge of the broad corruptions of his day. As he later wrote, he was managing editor of a newspaper that could not resist a payoff. R. A. Crothers owned the San Francisco *Bulletin,* a struggling marginal journal; and Crothers, like the great majority of newspaper owners in California at the time, was perfectly willing to take money anyhow and anywhere he could get it. William Herrin and the Southern Pacific Railroad that he represented were the great corrupters. "Country editors, many of them, were satisfied with an annual pass for the editor and his wife," Older wrote. "Some of the more important ones expected and got money for advertisements. Some of the metropolitan papers fared better, and among those was the *Bulletin*."

The *Bulletin* was on the Southern Pacific's payroll for $125 a month just to insure its "friendliness." The paper was also being paid off by the gas company and water companies, and Crothers was always eager to increase the size of these stipends. In the battle over the new muncipal charter, the Southern Pacific, which opposed it, raised the *Bulletin*'s "friendliness" fee from $125 to $250 a month, just to make certain that whatever support the paper might give the charter would be weak and ineffective.

Older, who had been a staunch supporter of Mayor Phelan and the new charter, fought a constant battle to preserve his own honor and the paper's despite Crothers' lack of principles. He succeeded at times, as in the municipal charter fight, by sneaking into the paper at the last minute a strong editorial endorsement that Crothers hadn't even seen; and at other times, he faced down his employer, threatening to quit when the paper's secret corruption became too much to stomach. But in the mayoralty election of 1901, Older had found himself powerless against Southern Pacific's money. The railroad, he later wrote, paid Crothers $7,500 to support the Republican candidate, and the kept paper performed the deed for which it had been bought.

The election left Older, who had wanted to support Schmitz's Democratic opponent, with a vile taste in his mouth. He had no illusions about Abe Ruef, convinced that Ruef would sell his soul to the highest bidder; and so, right after the election, he sent a message to Mayor Schmitz through the *Bulletin*'s business manager, a Schmitz follower. The burden of the message was this:

"If he [Schmitz] will be really true to Labor, to the people that elected him, and not associate himself with the evil forces in San Francisco, there is nothing that he cannot achieve politically in the United States. He can become Governor, he can become Senator, he can have a brilliant political career. Tell him that, and warn him against associating with Abraham Ruef, for Ruef will lead him astray."

Schmitz replied, as Older later wrote, that "Ruef was his friend and they were going to stand together." From that moment, Fremont Older became convinced that there was no hope. Sure that the new regime would be corrupt to the core, he set out on a years-long, relentless pursuit to track down the evidence that would justify his suspicions.

Older was right, but he could not know at the time just how right he was. When Schmitz took office on January 8, 1902, Ruef became the unpaid attorney for the mayor; and no sooner had this happened than big business corporations suddenly saw the wisdom of paying Abe Ruef handsome legal "retainers." One of the first in the act was the Pacific States Telephone and Telegraph Company. It had no pending court cases, but it fell all over itself in its eagerness to "retain" Ruef for his "advice" on municipal law at a fee of $250 a month—all in cash.

There was no way an outsider like Older could track down such cash deals, which, of course, were bribes cloaked in a thin tissue of legality. In the meantime, the colorful Mayor Schmitz cut a broad swath across the nation. He made a triumphal grand tour to the East. He was entertained by Theodore Roosevelt in the White House; he was honored at a reception given by the mayor of Chicago; he addressed the American Federation of Labor convention in New Orleans. In 1903 President Roosevelt visited San Francisco, and Schmitz, escorting him, basked in the reflected Presidential glory. The visit was a triumph for Schmitz, who, Ruef thought, really "had arrived"; and in another three-cornered race for mayor in November, 1903, Schmitz was re-elected by an even larger margin.

Fremont Older was almost beside himself. Day after day, the *Bulletin* thundered with charges of municipal corruption. By 1904 Schmitz had been in office long enough to have acquired a firm grip on the municipal bureaucracy. His appointees controlled the Board of Police Commissioners and the Board of Public Works. The police, of course, had complete sway over gambling and prostitution; they also issued liquor licenses. The Board of Public Works had authority over public buildings, the paving of streets, the issuance of construction permits. Schmitz put his brother, Herbert, on this key board. Older charged that Schmitz was a secret partner in the building firm run by his friend, Jerry Dineen, and that Herbert Schmitz refused building permits to other contractors, forcing them to employ the Dineen Building Company at much higher prices. Older also discovered that one firm had cheated the city out of thousands of dollars on a paving contract. Herbert Schmitz, he charged, had instructed the firm to do only part of the work contracted for, but to bill the city for the whole job.

Although Older kept crusading against the Ruef-Schmitz regime, Crothers, the owner of the *Bulletin,* didn't become personally involved until late one Saturday night in 1904. As he was leaving his office, a man who had evidently been lying in wait for him struck him over the head with an iron pipe. As Crothers fell, he was struck again. His cries for help brought passersby to his aid and scared off his assailant. The *Bulletin* promptly charged that the attack had been instigated by the Ruef ring.

The gingerly manner in which the official investigation was handled lent strength to this suspicion. The detective in charge of the case whitewashed the whole affair, reporting it was "a case of too many Scotch highballs." Crothers was infuriated. Yielding to the outraged cries of the *Bulletin,* the police commissioners broke the offending detective back to patrolman; but—or so the *Bulletin* charged —as soon as the heat occasioned by the affair had died down, Ruef had the man promoted to detective sergeant. This was just the first of many incidents of violence—some of them far more sensational— that were to mark the San Francisco scandal. Wary now, Crothers and Older both hired bodyguards, and the *Bulletin* stepped up its attacks.

As a result, it uncovered what Older dubbed the case of "the municipal crib." Insiders with influence in the administration had purchased an old Chinese opium den at 620 Jackson Street in the heart of Chinatown. They had the building condemned by the city, then obtained a permit from the obliging Board of Public Works for the construction of a three-storey lodging house on the site. The Dineen Building Company, naturally, got the permit to erect the new edifice.

When the structure was almost completed, a building inspector took a look at it and registered shock. The building was a rabbit-warren of tiny cubicles, not a full-sized room in the lot. "Why, this is not a lodging-house," exclaimed the inspector. "It is a whorehouse."

Herbert Schmitz pigeonholed the report and reprimanded the officious inspector. "The municipal crib" opened for business in May, 1904, and by November, the *Bulletin* was raising a tremendous outcry. "Gold Mine for Graft in Dive," it charged in a headline over one editorial. The *Bulletin* insisted the cubicles were being rented for $3 a shift to women occupants and that two shifts were employed for round-the-clock business. In January, 1905, the *Bulletin* roared:

"Gang Given a Brothel Corner." It charged police were closing down other houses of prostitution, driving business to "the municipal crib."

Older got the District Attorney and the grand jury interested. They raided the place and arrested seventy-two women. The women either refused to testify or told such baffling stories that the judge before whom they were brought for a hearing couldn't determine where the truth lay and went down to see for himself. He later reported: "While I cannot use that as evidence, I can and do . . . state the fact as I saw it on these premises. The condition was like that in a theater where you see a continuous stream of people going in and coming out."

The case was dismissed for lack of evidence, and it was not until 1907 that Older was vindicated for his suspicion that the Ruef-Schmitz combine had been pimping for the prostitutes. Then Ruef finally confessed that he had received one-quarter of the profits of "the municipal crib" and had split the payoff evenly with Mayor Schmitz.

Next came "the affair of the French restaurants." San Francisco was a prosperous, bustling city with a great number of high-quality restaurants and much dining out. The so-called French restaurants catered to all tastes in more ways than one. On their first floors were public dining rooms, serving fine food to some of the most distinguished families in the city. The second floors were devoted to luxuriously furnished private dining rooms, some of them equipped with convenient couches. And the third floors contained private supper-bedroom facilities, rented much like suites in the fanciest hotels. It was understood that respectable women satisfied the pangs of hunger on the first floor.

There were about a dozen French restaurants in the city, representing an investment of at least $1 million. To operate, they had to have liquor licenses; and these licenses, according to city regulation, had to be renewed every three months. In March, 1904, a Ruef police commissioner, Harry W. Hutton, voted against the renewal of the French restaurants' liquor licenses, charging they were luxurious houses of assignation. Mayor Schmitz, it was later disclosed, persuaded another commissioner, Thomas Reagan, to side with Hutton, and the votes of these two commissioners were enough to kill the liquor licenses.

Fremont Older learned about this brewing trouble one day when he went to dine at Marchand's, a famous French restaurant controlled by Pierre Priet. Pierre wore the long face of a man who has just come from his mother's funeral. Older inquired about his trouble.

"Mr. Older, I'm a ruined man," Pierre said. "They're going to put me out on the sidewalk after all these years building up this business."

Older didn't understand how "they" could do this. Pierre explained that all the French restaurants were to lose their liquor licenses when they came up for renewal in January, 1905. Older laughed and said jokingly: "Why don't you see Ruef?"

But Pierre was despondent. He was convinced that nothing could save him.

A few weeks later, a friend telephoned Older at the *Bulletin* office. He told the editor that the French restaurants had paid $10,000 "for protection" and their liquor licenses were to be renewed. Older rushed over to Marchand's.

He found Pierre seated at a side table, sipping black coffee and reading the *Chronicle,* the obvious picture of a man without cares.

"You look happy, Pierre," Older said.

"Yes, Mr. Older," Pierre replied. "My troubles are over. You know, when you are seek, send for the doctor. Well, and I send for the doctor—Dr. Ruef—and everything is all right."

Older dashed back to the *Bulletin* and splashed a headline across the top of the front page, charging a payoff in the French restaurants case. None of the other papers in the city seemed interested. Yet the maneuvers required to pay off on the payoff were so brazen that one would have thought they would have made even the most incurious eyebrow pop.

The trouble was that the two police commissioners who had taken such strong positions against the French restaurants felt it would be too embarrassing to do a flip-flop in public. Schmitz as mayor had the power under the new Phelan city charter to remove lesser public officials. So he now bounced Commissioner Hutton, charging him with living with a woman to whom he was not married. The mayor then filled the vacancy he had created with a stooge, and the police commissioners voted 2 to 1 to restore the French restaurants' liquor licenses.

The *Bulletin* denounced Schmitz, wondering what Hutton's private life had to do with his performance as police commissioner. And it flayed Abe Ruef in these words: "As a cheerful pirate, who does his deeds regardless of what the world thinks, Abe Ruef, landsman, rivals that eminent seaman, Captain Kidd."

Ruef struck back. Mayor Schmitz had been a newsboy in his youth, and he was a highly popular figure among the new generation of newsboys—a living example of the heights to which they might climb. Schmitz now turned his oratory on his young following and whipped them up to strike the *Bulletin*. Ruef, working through a group of gangsters who controlled the Newsboys Union, got this leadership to back the strike. The *Bulletin* could not be circulated. Older wrote: "Gangs cut the harness from the horses of the delivery wagons that we tried to get out. They stormed our drivers. Professional thugs broke the arms of loyal carriers, beat up our solicitors with brass knuckles. . . ."

The *Bulletin* was being strangled, but Older saw a way out. He summoned the "well-known tenderloin characters" who controlled the Newsboys Union and offered them $1,000 to call off the strike within twenty-four hours. They took the money, the strike ended, and, as a dividend, the bought-off gangsters got the newsboys to stage a hostile demonstration before Ruef's house.

Despite such minor setbacks, Ruef's power continued to grow. He ruled the Union Labor Party completely, and he had increasing influence in Republican ranks, working toward the happy day when he might successfully merge the two parties. With Mayor Schmitz running for re-election in the fall of 1905, the opposition became scared. Top Republican and Democratic leadership decided that the only way to beat Schmitz was to form a fusion ticket, uniting behind a single candidate. The outlook seemed dark for Ruef; so dismal, in fact, that he had difficulty putting a full slate of candidates in the field. In desperation, at the last moment, he filled the Board of Supervisors' slots with a hodge-podge of little-known men; and, hoping to get the votes of school teachers, he put up for District Attorney the non-political William H. Langdon, an attorney who had become superintendent of schools.

The anti-Ruef forces now went too far and created a backlash. Repressive employers formed the so-called Citizens' Alliance, an organization that was so rabidly anti-labor that it played into the hands of Ruef in a strong union city. Ruef made the most of the opportunity. He charged that the attacks upon Schmitz and himself were the products of a vicious anti-labor conspiracy; he denounced the *Bulletin* as the vehicle of a personal vendetta by Older.

The result stunned even Ruef and all but crushed Older. When the votes were counted on election night, November 7, 1905, it became clear that Ruef had scored a smashing, incredible victory. Schmitz had been re-elected by the largest margin ever. Langdon had polled nearly as many votes. And the entire Ruef slate of virtual unknowns for the Board of Supervisors had been swept into office by overwhelming margins.

"It was incredible to me," Older later wrote in his autobiography, *My Own Story*. ". . . I could not believe that the people of San Francisco had again chosen the Schmitz-Ruef crowd to rule the city. But they had."

Older went to bed "feeling that the world . . . was a hopeless place to live in." There followed two weeks of black despair during which he came to some conclusions about what had happened. It was clear to him that the public had not believed the *Bulletin*. The paper had screamed so loudly and so constantly about graft and corruption, with nothing ever proven, that the voters had bought Ruef's spite-work explanation. To overcome this stigma, Older was going to have to prove his charges in court.

Thinking along these lines, he recalled a pre-election speech by Francis J. Heney. Heney, a fighting cock who had grown up in one of the toughest districts in San Francisco, had become a federal prosecutor and had acquired a national reputation for exposing land frauds involving the illegal acquisitions of titles to government timber lands in California and Oregon. He had even sent a U.S. Senator from Oregon to prison. Just before the election, in a speech backing the fusion ticket, Heney had declared that he knew Ruef was corrupt; and he had predicted that, if Schmitz were re-elected, graft would become so bad "that the people of San Francisco will send for me in whatever part of the United States I am and beg me to come back here and put Ruef in the penitentiary where he belongs."

Recalling this, Fremont Older had his great inspiration. "If I could only get Heney—" he thought. "There was the French restaurant case. Certainly something could be done with that!"

Older decided to go to Washington. He would see President Roosevelt. He would try to get the President to free Heney and the famous Secret Service detective, William J. Burns, for an investigation of corruption in San Francisco.

Older's wife, Cora, and Crothers both thought "it was a crazy thing to do," but they humored him. "Sure, go ahead," they said in effect. "The trip will be good for you. You've been too wrought up about the election anyhow. It will give you a chance to calm down."

So Older went. He and Heney had luncheon in the Willard Hotel in Washington on December 2, 1905, and Older explained his plan. Heney made several suggestions. The kind of probe Older wanted, he said, could be conducted only through the office of the District Attorney; Langdon would have to deputize him to conduct it. Next, Heney said, he would absolutely have to have the services of William J. Burns, the detective who had been so invaluable to him in the land fraud cases. Burns, in turn, would have to build a detective force. All this would cost money. Heney didn't see how he could think of tackling the task with a budget of less than $100,000.

"Well, I'll take care of that. I'll arrange it," Older told him.

The next morning, the editor saw President Roosevelt in the White House. T.R., the reformer, was sympathetic. But he said he could not spare Heney and Burns at the moment. Perhaps, later. With this half-promise, Older returned to San Francisco.

The next day, he got a welcome shock. District Attorney Langdon walked into his office. Older had assumed that Langdon would be a creature of Ruef's. Langdon quickly set him straight. He picked up a copy of the penal code, looked Older in the eye and said: "My job is to enforce all the laws in that book. I mean to prosecute any man, whomever he may be, who breaks one of those laws. Any man. No matter what happens. Do you understand me?"

Older understood. Ruef, in hastily putting together a ticket he had never expected to win, had made the great blunder of his life. And in that whole big blunder, no single mistake was more crucial than the selection of a District Attorney whom he could not control.

From the moment of Langdon's visit, Older knew that he had a powerful ally. But he still had to raise that $100,000, and he went to the men who could afford to part with this kind of cash—the wealthy former mayor, Phelan, and Rudolph Spreckels, who had built a multimillion-dollar fortune in the sugar trade. Spreckels had distrusted Ruef ever since 1903 when Ruef had offered him a corrupt bargain in city bonds. An upright man and a fighter, Spreckels had been out-

raged and had felt ever since that he should work for political reform.
Now Older offered him the opportunity. And Spreckels, with Phelan
aiding, agreed to finance the Heney-Burns investigation.

In the meantime, Abe Ruef was discovering the dismaying costs
of his greatest victory. He was in command of a freebooting crew that
insisted on going off on its own and plundering everyone in sight. The
crude, untutored cast that Ruef had put in power on the Board of Supervisors had no conception of sophisticated corruption. Ruef was
horrified. He knew that he faced exposure and doom from the reck-
lessness of this ignorant band of cutthroats.

Trying to pound some sense into their skulls, he explained to
them just how the system must work if they were not all to wind up in
jail. None of them was to go off on free-lance hunts. The only graft
they would get would come through Ruef. He would keep half the
fees he was paid; the remaining half he would turn over to Supervisor
James L. Gallagher, a former city attorney and the most intelligent
man on the new board. Gallagher, in turn, would divide the money he
got from Ruef into eighteen equal shares for each of the supervisors.
This was the way it was going to be, Ruef said. They would vote as he
told them. They would be paid off in their split of his "attorney's
fees" later.

The mutinous crew yielded, muttering. But not even Abe Ruef
could keep them under control for long. Even Ruef's good friend,
Mayor Schmitz, became a problem. Schmitz was being wined and
dined, and given expensive gifts, by the well-placed and the powerful
who flattered him so much his head began to turn. In return for one
such series of favors, he browbeat the supervisors into approving a
franchise for a wealthy friend of his without any payoff. The pirate
crew grumbled. One of the more greedy, Andrew M. Wilson, was distinctly unhappy at having to trust Schmitz and Ruef for everything;
he itched to make his own deals.

Corruption now became cosmic. Everybody paid. Fight promoters, to get permits, gave Ruef "a fee" of $18,000. Pacific Gas and
Electric, to keep its high gas rates from being cut too drastically, paid
Ruef "a retainer" of $1,000 a month, and then, at his demand,
topped this with a special $20,000 "attorney's fee." A group of real
estate developers, known as the Parkside Realty Company, wanted a
new trolley line to run out to a suburban tract they hoped to develop.
They promised Ruef a $30,000 two-year "retainer," and actually paid

him the first $15,000. And so it went. The payoffs became ever more brazen.

Two cases, in the end, came to stand out above all the others: the telephone franchise case and the great overhead-trolley-line battle.

Pacific States Telephone and Telegraph, one of the first corporations to begin paying Ruef a cash "retainer" right after the first election of Schmitz, was the great Bell system giant in San Francisco. With the expiration of the Bell patents in 1893, however, a number of independent telephone companies had sprung up; and one of these, Home Telephone Company, of Toledo, Ohio, wanted to establish a competing system in San Francisco. Home hired Ruef as its attorney to get its franchise approved. His "fee" was to be $125,000, and he got $25,000 down.

Ruef kept this payment secret at the time, for excellent reasons. Pacific Telephone had had the foresight to raise his original $250 "retainer" to $1,000 a month; and when it sensed the danger from Home Telephone, it boosted this monthly stipend to $1,200. Ruef was thus in the position of taking money from both sides.

He was not the only one. Pacific Telephone, perhaps not certain that Ruef would stay bought, began a separate campaign to purchase the Board of Supervisors. Supervisor Wilson took the lead in arranging for this independent graft, violating Ruef's "only through me" order. In the end, Pacific Telephone bought up eleven of the supervisors for an outlay of $51,000.

Only then, too late, did Wilson begin to worry and let Ruef know about this freebooting accomplishment. There was a stormy session between Ruef and the supervisors. Ruef laid down the law: They were to vote for the Home Telephone franchise. On March 5, 1906, they did, but five of those who had been paid off by Pacific abstained from voting.

Theodore V. Halsey, the payoff agent of Pacific, telephoned Ruef, roaring that he had been "double-crossed." Ruef asked blandly, just as if it was all news to him: "You don't mean to tell me that your company paid those supervisors money for their votes?"

"Certainly," said Halsey, practically jumping up and down at the other end of the telephone. "And you know it!"

Ruef agreed to see if he could get the supervisors to pay back at least *half* of the bribes that failed—but they wouldn't. Ruef later confessed that, when he collected his Home Telephone "fee," he gave

Gallagher $62,000 in cash to be divided among the supervisors, gave $30,000 to Schmitz, and kept the remaining $33,000 for himself.

It had been a highly profitable transaction, but Ruef's juiciest deal was still to come.

Most of the streetcar lines in San Francisco had been bought up by Eastern investors and consolidated into the United Railroads of San Francisco. This corporation was headed by Patrick Calhoun, the grandson of the famous pre-Civil War Senator from South Carolina, John C. Calhoun. Patrick Calhoun was a hard man, six feet tall with pale blue, steel-like eyes and a mouth that bit downward at the corners. A drooping white mustache seemed almost out of place in a face so stern and harsh.

United Railroads had been over-capitalized by Calhoun through the issuance of $75 million worth of stocks and bonds on properties valued at only about $39 million. Calhoun soon saw that he could earn a profit on this inflated capital structure by just two methods: beating down labor's demands for wage increases and modernizing a system that was a hodge-podge of cable cars, overhead trolleys, horse cars, and even ancient steam engines. Calhoun especially desired to convert cable cars to trolley cars except on a few of the very steepest hills.

Such changes would need the approval of the city administration, and, as early as 1902, United Railroads had begun to pay Ruef a secret fee, in cash, of $500 a month as a "special consulting attorney." The payoffs were made by Tirey L. Ford, who was Attorney General of California even after becoming chief counsel for United Railroads.

After Ruef's landslide victory of 1905, United suddenly doubled his "retainer" to $1,000 a month—all cash. Ford also sought Ruef's help in getting approval of an overhead trolley system. He suggested this might be worth an "extra fee" of $50,000. Ruef protested that United should be ashamed to offer such a paltry sum. Businessmen back East would pay much more for such help, he said, and he asked for $250,000. He and Ford eventually agreed on $200,000.

This was the way matters stood when a twenty-eight-second earthquake at 5:14 A.M. Wednesday, April 18, 1906, destroyed most of San Francisco. Buildings toppled, gas lines and water mains were broken, electric wires came tumbling down. Fires sprang up everywhere as if by magic, quickly raged out of control, and swept onward in great walls of flame, engulfing most of the city. Before it was over, more than four square miles of the city had been reduced to charred, smoking rubble, more than 500 lives had been lost, and property damage was estimated at from $250 to $300 million, a stupendous sum in the uninflated currency of the day.

The disaster gave Mayor Schmitz his finest hour. He took charge with an energy and competence few had imagined he possessed. He appointed a Citizens' Committee of Fifty, composed of the city's leading figures, to deal with the multiple problems caused by the quake. In doing so, he completely bypassed the incompetent Board of Supervisors. He worked almost around the clock, day after day, making emergency arrangements for food, clothing and shelter for the thousands left destitute. So remarkable was his performance that even the *Bulletin* stopped its attacks, and Schmitz wore the hero's halo.

But in spite of the city-wide wreckage, the wheeling and dealing went on. Patrick Calhoun saw the disaster as a boon. Street transportation would have to be restored; the quickest way to do this would be by converting to overhead trolleys—and so United Railroads pressed home its demands.

Opposition folded. Both Spreckels and Phelan had been opposed to United's plan, contending that there was danger in stringing overhead electric wires above the streets and that safer underground conduits should be used. But in the face of the devastated city's desperate need for restored transportation, Calhoun and United had their way. Only William Randolph Hearst's *Examiner,* long partial to Schmitz, attacked the deal. It conceded that trolleys were needed at the moment, but argued that this should have been only a temporary expedient. The ordinance giving United blanket power to do as it wished was so wrong, the *Examiner* wrote, that "it smacks and smells of bribery and of a ghoulish effort to steal from the city in her time of need."

It did, indeed. For in the midst of the acres of blackened ruins, bribery flourished. Calhoun had transferred $200,000 from the East to the U.S. Mint in San Francisco. This was turned over to Tirey Ford. And Ruef, who had been dashing all around the city in rescue efforts, as had Schmitz, drove in his car to Ford's office to pick up the heavy money bags.

He later confessed that he gave Gallagher $85,000 to split among the supervisors. Gallagher kept $15,000 for himself. Wilson, ever greedy, demanded and got $10,000. The rest of the supervisors had to be consoled with $4,000 each. According to Ruef, he later paid Schmitz $50,000, keeping $65,000 for himself.

Ruef was now at the height of his political power, but there were breakers ahead. The investigation that Older had engineered was under way. William J. Burns' detectives were hard at work; they followed Ruef everywhere and burrowed into his numerous transactions.

The corruption was now so blatant it could not be concealed. The supervisors, their pockets jingling with more money than they had ever possessed, were like sailors who had just hit port. One opened an expensive new saloon. Another, a former hack driver, went off on an extended trip to Chicago. A third, who had been the driver of a delivery wagon, suddenly announced plans to take his wife and children on a tour of Ireland. Schmitz himself departed on October 1 for a trip to Europe, leaving Gallagher as acting mayor. And San Francisco soon heard that its chief executive had occupied one of the most expensive suites in New York's plush Waldorf-Astoria Hotel and that he was cavorting around Europe in a style befitting "a newly created Nevada millionaire."

In this atmosphere, news of the Heney-Burns probe broke. On October 20, 1906, District Attorney Langdon named Heney his deputy to conduct the investigation, and the *Bulletin* disclosed that Burns' detectives were already at work. Since both Heney and Burns were national heroes, the twin announcements created a sensation in San Francisco.

Ruef retaliated with an action born of desperation. The city charter gave the mayor, with the approval of the Board of Supervisors, the power to remove any city official. Ruef now forced Acting Mayor Gallagher and the subservient board to oust Langdon as district attorney and name him to the post instead.

Fremont Older, then living in San Rafael, had gone to bed when he got the news in a late-night telephone call from Rudolph Spreckels. "What!" he exclaimed. "This is incredible." But Spreckels insisted it was so, and Older began to make plans. By eleven o'clock the next morning, he had 20,000 copies of a *Bulletin* extra on the streets, describing what had happened and urging the public to turn out en masse in protest against a move that would have put Ruef in charge of the investigation of Ruef.

Heney and Hiram W. Johnson, a rising young lawyer whom Spreckels had engaged to assist in the probe, worked through the night preparing an application for an injunction to bar Ruef from seizing the D.A.'s office. The hearing was scheduled before Judge Thomas F. Graham at two P.M., and by that time the *Bulletin* extra had done its work. Thousands of citizens poured out and surrounded the synagogue that, as a result of the fire, had become a temporary courtroom. Traffic was blocked. "The crowds surged this way and that, cheering, hooting and yelling; dangerous, in a mood for anything," Older later wrote. Judge Graham arrived, passed through the mass, heard the angry mutterings—and upheld Langdon as District Attorney. Ruef's gamble had failed; the probe went on.

A new grand jury was sworn in, headed by B. P. Oliver, a real estate dealer. It became known as "the Oliver grand jury," and it quickly voted indictments against Ruef and Schmitz in the French restaurant bribery case. But that was, for the moment, almost all that the jury could produce. As Heney later said: "From October, 1906, until March 8, 1907, we labored every day trying to get evidence. . . . For five long weary months, we labored until midnight after midnight, and sometimes until two or three o'clock in the morning, struggling to work out a case."

Then came a break. Ruef had split with two of his political supporters, Frank Maestretti and Golden M. Roy. Maestretti had been president of the Board of Public Works, and Schmitz, in one of his last acts before taking off for Europe, had fired him. Older moved at once. He talked to both Maestretti and Roy, hoping to get them to turn on Ruef, but, at first, neither would talk. Burns kept after them and came to the conclusion that Roy was the one who had the most information about the Ruef ring's payoffs.

Older discussed the situation with Spreckels; he was excited about the possibility of a big break-through. Spreckels was dubious. "Can you trust them?" he asked.

"Well," Older answered, "unfortunately, Rudolph, the crimes that were committed here were not known to respectable people like Bishop Nichols or our leading prelates. If we are going to get anywhere, we've got to get our information from crooks."

Older now dreamed up a scheme to break down Roy. Burns, as soon as he met Roy, had recognized him as a man whose real name was Moritz Roy Golden. This Golden had fled from Guthrie, Oklahoma, ten years previously, charged with forging the name of the Secretary of the Interior on a letter appointing him Indian agent. Roy's wife and children, whom he loved, knew nothing of this episode in his past. Older now prepared a full-page article, adorned with pictures, exposing Roy. He had it set in type, had proofs pulled, and then summoned Roy to his office. He handed the exposé to Roy and told him: "Read it all."

As Roy began to read, his face paled, and he reeled on his feet.

"What do you want me to do?" he asked.

"I want you to tell the truth," Older replied.

"All right," Roy said. "I'm willing to tell you the truth—everything."

There were conflicting versions about what happened next; but, according to Older, who should have known, Ruef got suspicious and moved against Maestretti and Roy. The two owned a large and popular skating rink, the Dreamland Rink, and there had been rumors that young girls were being seduced there. Taking advantage of this gossip, Ruef had an ordinance introduced that would have barred girls under eighteen going to the rink unless accompanied by their mothers—a law that would have put Dreamland out of business. According to Older, it was Roy himself, not Detective Burns, who later claimed the credit, who devised an ingenious plot to trap the supervisors. Roy would bribe them with Burns himself watching.

Three tiny peepholes were drilled through a door connecting Roy's office at the rink with an adjoining room and Roy rehearsed the whole scene. It seemed to Older "too much of a melodrama," but Roy reassured him, saying: "Don't worry. It will happen exactly as we have planned it."

And indeed, two days later, Supervisor Tom Lonergan sat in a chair that had been placed directly in front of the peepholes and was observed taking $500 from Roy, promising that, in return, he would vote to kill the skating rink ordinance. Soon two other supervisors were seen accepting similar bribes. Then the trap was sprung.

Langdon and Heney grilled the supervisors, and they began to talk. The whole story of the Ruef ring's briberies and payoffs soon came tumbling out. The prosecutors were willing to offer the supervisors immunity to get the testimony they needed to convict Ruef and, hopefully, the men behind Ruef—men like Tirey Ford, Patrick Calhoun, and William F. Herrin. Gallagher and the other supervisors, grabbing at this life-line, testified before the grand jury. And indictments poured out, some of them against highly placed businessmen like Theodore V. Halsey, the Pacific Telephone executive who had bribed the supervisors. Shudders began to run through the circles of the elite.

Almost all of San Francisco had been united behind the graft investigation as long as only the rascally politicians were its targets. However, the instant it became clear that the probers would not be content to stop there, but were actually going after the big money men who had paid the bribes, the atmosphere changed. Older and others among the crusaders began to be treated as though they had leprosy.

Into this super-charged atmosphere stepped Patrick Calhoun. He recognized that he was in danger the instant the grand jury began to churn out indictments. Then there occurred a municipal disaster from which he would be able to emerge as the city's shining hero.

For months the streetcar workers had been seeking higher wages. An arbitrator had recommended a settlement that did not entirely satisfy them. Agitation for a strike began, led by a man by the name of Bowling. Bowling worked on the men and prevailed. On May 5, 1907, the union struck, precipitating the longest and most violent streetcar strike in American history.

Traffic in the city was paralyzed for days, and the outrage of the business classes knew no bounds. Here was a city devastated by fire and earthquake—and here also were those greedy union men, striking, taking callous advantage of the city's misery. When Calhoun imported hordes of strike-breakers, San Franciscans hailed him as their deliverer. He "rode up and down Market Street, to the admiration of all who saw him," Older later wrote.

The strike lasted until December and resulted in the crushing of the Carmen's Union, which surrendered its charter. Calhoun emerged from the crisis as the white knight who had "saved" San Francisco. And Bowling, the corrupt union leader, went on the payroll of United Railroads.

Coinciding with the start of the strike was the confession of Abe Ruef on May 7. This came only after long negotiations. Spreckels had been willing to grant Ruef complete immunity in return for testimony against the business bribe-payers who, in his mind, were the real culprits. But Heney wouldn't stand for this. Ruef, he said, was "the greatest rascal" of the bunch, and "to let Ruef go free of all punishment under the circumstance would be a crime against society." Ruef might, Heney agreed, be given leniency or even full immunity later if he testified fully and truthfully. As for Ruef himself, he had to be satisfied with this bargain, and he began to tell the grand jury what he knew.

Tirey Ford was indicted; Calhoun was indicted; Schmitz himself went to trial. On June 13, 1907, a trial jury convicted Schmitz of extortion, and he was sentenced to serve five years in San Quentin. This was the first great victory, but it was to be only temporary. Schmitz's conviction was overturned on appeal, and in the end he went free.

The spate of indictments, however, now provoked a series of ever more violent clashes. When Heney tried Tirey L. Ford for passing along to Ruef the $200,000 sent from the East by Calhoun, the "hero" of the San Francisco streetcar strike threw all of his enormous resources into the battle. Calhoun had to save Ford to save himself, and the evidence is that, literally, he stopped at nothing.

A battery of the highest-priced lawyers money could hire, headed by the famous Earl Rogers of Los Angeles, defended Ford. An army of private detectives invaded the city. The San Francisco *Call* wrote that, behind the legal battery, there trooped "a motley train of gun fighters, professional pluguglies, decoys, disreputable 'detectives,' thugs, women of the half world, and the wolfish pack of gutter journalism."

Fremont Older became a special target. As he later wrote: "I never left my office that one or two men did not follow me to my hotel . . . all sorts of traps were set to catch me." Women would telephone him and tell him that, if he came to a certain hotel room, they would give him invaluable information. Such frameups were too obvious, and he avoided them. But he could not avoid everything.

Older and his wife, ostracized now by the "best" people of the city—to the extent that Older resigned from the Bohemian Club— had formed the habit of going to the beach late in the day. They had rented a tiny bungalow attached to a restaurant run by a Mrs. Gunn, and their one relief from the mounting pressures of the case was to take a swim in the ocean at sunset and then have a leisurely dinner in the restaurant. One evening, as Older was leaving his office, "a very good friend of mine, who had deep connections in the underworld, passed by me and said warningly: 'Keep away from the beach.' "

Older was disturbed. He knew the warning was important. But he was determined not to give up the one form of recreation he had left. And so he got two police department plainclothesmen to follow his wife and himself. The policemen sat in their car, watchful while the Olders took their nightly swim. "Later," Older wrote "I learned that Calhoun's men had employed a half-breed Mexican gunfighter to come from Arizona to San Francisco to 'get' me." The Mexican had been watching in front of the *Bulletin* one day when another gunfighter who knew him asked what he was doing. The half-breed replied that he was waiting to see Older so he could recognize him and shoot him on the beach. "The man to whom the Mexican gave his confidence was a friend of the man who warned me," Older later wrote. "I had done favors for both of them and they didn't want any harm to come to me. So the warning was given me."

True, this plot had been foiled, but for Patrick Calhoun this was only the beginning. He had brought Luther Brown from Los Angeles to head his detective force, and he attempted to bribe Golden Roy. Calhoun wanted Roy to implicate Older, Spreckels, and Heney for themselves taking bribes. Roy kept the prosecution informed. At one point, Calhoun offered him $80,000 for his cooperation, but backed off after his attorneys told him he might be walking into a trap. Later Calhoun and Brown worked on Roy to get him to sign an affidavit charging that Burns, Heney, Gallagher, and Older had all been bribed by Spreckels. As Roy was leaving after this conference, Luther Brown casually passed him $3,000 as a small token of goodwill—and Roy immediately turned the money over to the prosecution.

Roy pretended to Calhoun and Brown that he was afraid to sign an affidavit under oath. Couldn't they take his "confession" in the form of a statement instead? They agreed. Roy brought the statement to Older, who had it copied and put in Phelan's safe. Then Roy took the original document back to Luther Brown. Pretending to be worried, he said, "Now this is not to be used until I give my consent. Is that right?" Brown replied, "Yes, I'll agree to that."

"Very well, then, just write that down at the bottom and sign it," Roy said. And Brown obliged. Roy carried the statement back, and it went into Heney's safe.

But Roy made one mistake. He showed the signed statement to his attorney. And Calhoun learned of it almost instantly. That leak ruined everything.

Still the web of plot and counterplot continued to weave its way in ever more sinister patterns. Patrick Calhoun was still determined to "get" Older. One day during the trial of Tirey Ford, Older received a mysterious telephone call from a "Mr. Stapleton," who said he had some "very important information" to give Older if Older would come to his room at the Savoy Hotel. Older, who was in Heney's office at the time, recognized that this might be a trap—but, then, it might not be. He decided to go. He left Heney's office and started to walk along Van Ness Avenue toward the Savoy. An automobile with four "pretty tough characters" pulled up at the curb, and two of them jumped out. One who was "very pale and nervous" flourished a warrant under Older's nose. It accused him of criminal libel and had been issued by a Justice of the Peace in Los Angeles—a man who owed his position to Luther Brown.

The men herded Older into the car. He told them he wanted to see his lawyer and arrange bail. They said they were taking him to a judge's chambers, but they didn't. The car kept right on going out of town, picking up speed. Older realized it was a trap and tried to rise in the car to attract the attention of passersby or a policeman. The man beside him in the back seat pulled him down, pressed a pistol against his side and told him: "If you make any attempt to escape I'll shoot you."

Older felt certain then that he was going to be assassinated. He saw another car ahead of the one in which he and his kidnappers were riding. In it were Luther Brown, the head of Calhoun's detective force, and Porter Ashe, a Calhoun lawyer. Desperately, Older began to talk. He directed his words primarily at "a dark man" on the front seat of the car, a man who looked to him "like a sport." He said he realized this was a United Railroads job. It was natural they should hate him because he had been fighting them pretty hard. "But this kind of deal isn't fair," he added. "It isn't sportsmanlike. They are dealing the cards from under the table."

Despite Older's appeal, the kidnappers hurried Older aboard a train, the *Los Angeles Lark,* and imprisoned him in a compartment. That night, they took him out to the dining car to eat, and he continued to work on the "dark man," saying he didn't ask any mercy for himself, but he didn't think it fair to make his wife suffer by not letting her know what had happened to him. Finally, the dark man shoved a telegram blank at him and said: "By God, you write a telegram to her or to anyone you like, and I'll file it at San José." This plan was foiled, however, when Luther Brown intercepted the telegram and tore it up.

The next morning, when the train stopped at Santa Barbara, Older looked out the window and was amazed to see practically the whole town crowding the station platform. There was a rap on the stateroom door. One of the two constables who had been guarding him opened it—and was promptly served with a subpoena.

Older and his kidnappers were driven to the courthouse, where Older learned that Heney and Spreckels had obtained a writ for his release. But how had they known about his plight, about where he was being taken?

It turned out that a young lawyer had been in the dining car the previous evening when Older was eating. Porter Ashe and Luther Brown were seated at another table, adjoining the young lawyer's. The latter overheard enough of their conversation to understand that they planned to spirit someone off the train at San Luis Obispo and take him for "a run through the mountains," where, as Older later learned, he was to have been killed. The young lawyer overheard enough to make him suspect a murder plot, and he followed Ashe outside the dining car and asked: "Whom have you got?" Whereupon Ashe replied: "We've got Fremont Older."

Alarmed, the lawyer left the train at Salinas at one o'clock in the morning, though he had intended to ride through to Los Angeles, and telephoned the San Francisco *Call,* telling the newspaper what he had learned and what he feared. Spreckels and Heney were notified and both went to work drafting the order to free Older.

The two constables who had guarded Older turned state's evidence, and a grand jury indicted both Ashe and Brown for the kidnaping. Brown was tried a year later—and was acquitted. The charges against Ashe were dropped. This was typical. It was now becoming almost impossible to convict anyone of anything, so drastically had the atmosphere of the city changed once the businessmen who had paid bribes for special favors realized that they might be next on the firing line.

Tirey Ford was tried twice. Heney attempted to win his case without putting Ruef on the stand because he thought Ruef had played him false by insisting the $200,000 he had received had always been discussed as "a fee" and that the dirty word "bribe" had not passed the lips of anyone. Very probably if hadn't, for in sophisticated circles there is a mutual understanding about the purposes of such considerate donations; the mechanics don't have to be spelled out.

Heney, it seems, should have been able to get this idea across to the jury through Ruef's testimony, regardless of how far Ruef wanted to go. But Heney was angry with the man who should have been his star witness and kept him off the stand. He had other difficulties, too. Supervisors Michael W. Coffey and Wilson suddenly developed such bad memories that they were worthless as prosecution witnesses, and Heney charged that they had been "reached" by Calhoun's agents. The result was that, at the first trial of Ford, the jury disagreed after thirty ballots. A second trial ended on December 3, 1907, with Ford's acquittal.

San Francisco was now split into two hostile camps. The reformers had lost most of their support and were now backed only by a dwindling segment of idealists and common people who could not be reached or influenced. The opposition was increasingly formidable. Labor was opposed to the prosecution because it had convicted Schmitz, labor's mayor. And the wealthy and respectable, the "best" people, were positively vicious. Wealthy depositers withdrew their money from Spreckels' First National Bank. Large mercantile establishments quit advertising in the *Bulletin*. Oliver, who had had the misfortune to head the indicting grand jury, was boycotted by clients and former clients and forced out of his once-prosperous real estate business. Mrs. Older commented that, in social circles, "women reserved their sweetest smiles for the candidates for the state's prisons."

In this climate, Heney decided to bring Ruef to trial, arguing that he had not been truthful enough or helpful enough to deserve consideration. Almost at once, violence took on a new dimension.

A key witness against Ruef, obviously, would be Supervisor Gallagher. He was the man to whom Ruef had passed the money, the man who knew what the money was for, and the man who divided it up with the other supervisors. And so an attempt was made to murder Gallagher.

On April 22, 1908, a shattering dynamite explosion blew in the whole front of the house in which Gallagher was living. It seemed a miracle that neither Gallagher nor anyone in his family was injured. Heney and Spreckels denounced the outrage as the work of "hired assassins," and a cartoon in the *Call,* according to Walton Bean, who has written the fullest account of the Ruef ring exposure, "showed a group of bloated millionaires in a room in their club, one of them touching his cigar to the end of a fuse leading through the door."

This first dynamite blast, just in case Supervisor Gallagher was so dense as not to get the message, was followed by a second. On May 26 a similar explosion wrecked three residential buildings which Gallagher and a partner had recently constructed. It was abundantly evident that somebody was trying to intimidate Supervisor Gallagher, and logic said that "somebody" had to be connected with the Ruef-Calhoun defense forces that were now welded together in a pact of mutual self-preservation.

A few weeks later this logical suspicion became a virtual certainty. A young Greek, John Claudianes, was arrested in Chicago and confessed that he had planted the bombs. He said his brother, Peter, who also confessed, had hired him. Peter said he had been engaged for the bloody deed by still a third Greek, Felix Paduvaris, who by this time had fled back to Europe and was never apprehended.

Investigations of Paduvaris' background disclosed this much: He had had ties to both Ruef and United Railroads. He had been a labor employment agent, a usurer, and a minor politician. United Railroads had employed him as "a spotter." In his political role, he was credited with having delivered "the Greek vote" and most of the law business of the Greek community to Ruef. Furthermore, Peter Claudianes, while doing a life sentence in San Quentin, later told Fremont Older that there had been a plan to blow him up at his beach cottage at the same time Gallagher's house was dynamited. Paduvaris, Claudianes said, had rented the cottage next to Older's on the beach and had stored in it fifteen pounds of dynamite, but the presence of the plainclothesmen who had protected Older and his wife during their swims had scared off the dynamiters.

This was the kind of deadly, no-holds-barred opposition with which the prosecution was struggling, and the "good" citizens of San Francisco couldn't have cared less. The first trial of Ruef ended in another hung jury, split six to six after forty-three hours of deliberation.

Heney was convinced that several members of the jury had been fixed. He was also convinced that he, Spreckels, and Burns had been marked for assassination in a conspiracy hatched among the wealthy and powerful forces of San Francisco.

Passions, already white hot, intensified further as Heney brought Ruef to trial for a second time. After the Gallagher dynamiting, a Citizens League for Justice was formed, and its 200 members helped Burns' detectives check up on prospective jurors. As a result, two of Ruef's lawyers were implicated in a plot to bribe a prospective juror by promising him $1,000 if he got on the second Ruef jury and voted for an acquittal. The go-between in this deal, a building contractor, ultimately confessed and spent four years in prison; but the two attorneys who had masterminded the attempt were acquitted. You just didn't convict men of such fine social standing in San Francisco.

In this atmosphere, it took seventy-two days just to pick a jury for Ruef's second trial, involving the $200,000 United Railroads bribery. Heney, fighting to get a clean jury in a city where bribe money was flowing like wine, grilled some of the prospective jurors severely. He focused on one, Morris Haas, for a very good and specific reason. Older later wrote: "This man was an ex-convict, and the lover of a married woman. One day he boasted to her that he was to be on the Ruef jury, and that he was to get several thousand dollars out of it. She repeated this to her husband; and he, furious with rage and jealous of Haas, sent the information to District Attorney Langdon."

When Haas was placed in the jury box, the judge asked him if there was any reason why he should not serve. Haas replied that there was not. Heney then exposed his past criminal record, and Haas was dismissed. He felt ashamed and humiliated. And as time went on— and, according to Older, as United Railroads detectives taunted him and whipped up his passions—he became venomous.

On Nov. 13, 1908, the first testimony in Ruef's second trial was taken. About 4:30 in the afternoon a recess was called. Heney stood at the prosecution table talking to his aides. There were some 200 persons in the room at the time, but no one paid particular attention to the nondescript little man who sidled down the aisle toward the prosecution table. There he paused, suddenly whipped out a pistol— and fired a bullet into Heney's head from a distance of a few inches.

The bullet had pierced Heney's skull just to the front of the right ear. He crashed to the floor like a man-poleaxed, and everyone in the courtroom assumed that he was dead. Pandemonium broke out. The gunman, Morris Haas, was seized on the spot.

Newspapers flooded the streets with extras. "Crowds gathered on the streets and in the hotels, the air was electric," Older wrote. ". . . San Francisco's mood was dangerous that night, and the slightest impetus would have precipitated the crowds into mobs, ready for lynching."

If Heney had died, the city almost certainly would have been ripped apart—but miraculously Heney lived. He had happened to be laughing when he was shot, and so the bullet passed between his jaws and lodged in the jaw muscles under his left ear. The slightest deviation in its course would have been fatal. As it was, Heney lost all hearing in his right ear, but he did survive. And Hiram Johnson took over the prosecution.

The trial continued in an atmosphere of seemingly unending melodrama. Detective Burns kept questioning Haas in prison, trying to get a confession from him, trying to find out who had instigated the assassination attempt; but Burns was frustrated. On the evening of November 14, while under guard in his cell, Haas suddenly whipped out a small Derringer pistol and blew his brains out.

The graft prosecution was almost beside itself. How had Haas managed to get such a weapon in prison? Both Burns and Police Captain Thomas Duke had searched him thoroughly and were convinced he had no weapon on him when he was placed in his cell. Burns, who believed he could have proved Haas had been hired to assassinate Heney had Haas lived, was almost wild with fury. He and the press accused Police Chief William J. Biggy with having "arrayed himself" on the side of the defense.

The city was shaken with demands that Biggy resign, and the police chief, much disturbed, boarded a police launch one foggy night to make a trip across the bay to the home of a police commissioner in Belvedere. The commissioner persuaded him not to resign; and Biggy, apparently in better spirits, boarded the launch for the trip back. He never made it. His body was found floating in the bay two days later.

Was it suicide? Or murder? San Francisco never found out. Supposedly, the only other man on the police launch at the time was the pilot, William Murphy. He insisted he knew nothing. Two years later, when he was committed to an insane asylum, he was still muttering that he didn't know what had happened, that he had had nothing to do with Chief Biggy's death.

In this climate of attempted assassination, suicide, mysterious death, the trial of Ruef finally came to an end. Hiram Johnson had handled the prosecution brilliantly, laying the foundation for a political career that was to make him nationally famous. As the trial came to a close, Burns reported to Johnson that he had information that four of the jurors had been fixed. Johnson made dramatic and extra-legal use of this information. In his closing summation to the jury, he called each of the four by name, pointed an accusing finger and stared each in the face as he thundered:

"YOU, you DARE NOT acquit this man!"

In the end, they didn't dare. Ruef was convicted December 10, 1908, and was sentenced to serve fourteen years in San Quentin Prison.

It was the last and the only real victory of the sensational corruption probe. With the "best" classes leading the way, San Francisco voters swept the crusaders out of office in the election of 1909. Heney, running for District Attorney, was defeated by a candidate who had promised, in effect, to drop all pending cases if he were elected. He was. And he did.

Supervisor Gallagher, a key witness in the still pending indictments against Patrick Calhoun, simply got lost. It was rumored he had gone into hiding somewhere in Vancouver, British Columbia. In any event, he stayed out of reach until all of the indictments against Calhoun and the other utility executives had been dismissed. Then, his mission accomplished, he returned to San Francisco.

"It was over," Older wrote, "and we had just one thing to show for it—Ruef in jail. Of all of the men who had bought and sold San Francisco, we had put just one behind bars, in stripes."

The exposure of the Abe Ruef ring and the graft prosecution that followed were probably the most dramatic events of their kind in American history. And they illustrated many truths—and not very happy truths—about the American people and the American political boss system.

The first was a truth that Lincoln Steffens found time and time again in the study he called *The Shame of the Cities*. The American people, he wrote, theoretically want good government. But only theoretically. As soon as the shoe began to pinch, as soon as investigations touched the wealthy, as soon as businesses could not work the special deals that made money, or the common man could not fix an annoying minor ticket, then Steffens found that the crusading prosecutor or reformer became a prophet without honor in his home territory. He often made a great reputation for himself by his cleanup campaign; he would be hero in the state or nation. But to be elected to anything he would have to run for governor or U.S. Senator, appealing to a larger public that, theoretically, was for good government and did not yet realize the cost of uprightness.

Hiram Johnson was a prime example of this. California cheered this brilliant prosecutor who had put Abe Ruef in prison; and so, at a time when Johnson could probably not have been elected dog catcher in San Francisco, he was elected governor of California. As governor, Johnson headed a progressive revolt in the state that in time ended the overweening influence of the Southern Pacific Railroad; then he went on to a multi-termed career in the U.S. Senate. But San Francisco, where he had made his reputation, wanted no more truck with reformers.

The saddest repudiation was perhaps that of Heney. This hardworking prosecutor, who had almost lost his life in the cause, had accepted not a penny of pay for three years. He had met his own living expenses out of money he had saved. "He finished the fight almost without funds, his practice gone, and with nothing but defeat at the hands of the people of San Francisco to repay him for it all," Older wrote. Boycotted by all the wealthy and big business interests, Heney had to move his law office to Los Angeles. He had a national reputation. He was a national hero. But he could not make a living in San Francisco.

Roy, the skating rink proprietor whose clever scheme had broken the graft case wide open, was ruined. He, too, was boycotted. His restaurant failed, his skating rink failed, he lost all his money. He disappeared from San Francisco, and, for a time, according to Older, "not even his family knew where he was." Roy went back East, found employment, built up some capital again, and later returned to California, becoming a prosperous businessman—but not in San Francisco, in San José.

The rascals fared much better. Schmitz brashly re-entered politics. He ran for mayor again in 1915, and, though he was defeated, 35,000 voted for him. Then, in 1917, he made another race, this time for the Board of Supervisors! And this time he was elected, beginning a series of two-year terms.

One of the most curious aspects of the case was the attitude of some of the reformers themselves. Lincoln Steffens adhered to the theory that men were not "good" or "bad," only the system was "bad," and this made men act the way they did. Steffens was on the inside of many of the prosecution's councils of war, and he continually advocated exposure without punishment. Show up the system, punish no one, he urged. He met Patrick Calhoun and liked him. Calhoun, he found, was a "realist," "an old, American gentlemen," a man "of intelligence" who "knew what he was about."

Strangely enough, Fremont Older, the passionate crusading editor, began to have second thoughts along similar lines. It seemed unfair to him that Abe Ruef should be the lone scapegoat, and he began to feel that Ruef had not been treated with complete fairness by Heney. So he turned around and began a campaign to get Ruef released from prison. After serving four years and seven months, Ruef was indeed paroled on August 21, 1915, and in time he returned to San Francisco and went back into the real estate business.

Is one to conclude, then, that it is just "the system?" This is what one finds hardest to buy about the philosophy of Lincoln Steffens. All systems, whatever they are, are composed of men, and men by their actions make them whatever they become. It is those actions that count; and, if men are to have stature above the animal level, they must have responsibility for their deeds—and be judged accordingly.

One is compelled to ask: What men and forces were responsible for the steadily increasing tempo of violence in San Francisco—for the dynamitings, for the kidnaping of Fremont Older, for the plot to assassinate him at his beach house, for the bribing of jurors? And what about the attempt to assassinate Heney and the mysterious suicide, so convenient perhaps for others, of Morris Haas? Isn't it obvious that Ruef and Calhoun and their army of hirelings were behind such violent, murderous deeds?

And still another series of questions:

Is there, then, no difference between men like Fremont Older and Rudolph Spreckels and Francis Heney—men who risked their fortunes and their lives to expose a corrupt regime—and men like Abe Ruef and Patrick Calhoun, men of education and wealth and ability, who were so greedy and so ambitious that they would stop at nothing? And if there is a difference, as most assuredly there is, should there be no recognition of that difference, no punishment?

San Francisco never faced up to those questions and their implicit answers. Unfortunately, in most instances, America has not faced up to them either. It is a truism of the American political boss system, often so riddled with corruption, that exposure brings only the jailing of a scapegoat, a Tweed or a Ruef; that others equally guilty are protected; that the American public quickly wearies of the hardships of reform and yearns for a return of the fix; and that, in many instances, the honest prosecutors of corruption suffer, and scoundrels like Schmitz become, with the passage of years, admired for their flair and their brass.

Unless such basic attitudes change, the boss system threatens to endure forever—and with it, corruption.

6

---◆◆◆---

The Most Boss-Ridden
State—New Jersey

NEW JERSEY HAS the well-deserved reputation of being the most
boss-ridden state in the American nation. For more than fifty
years, from 1917 to 1972, its political life was dominated by two
bosses whose influence was not confined to a single city or county, but
whose long reach extended across the state and determined, among
other things, who should occupy the governor's chair in Trenton.

This relatively small state tells much, then, about the political
boss system when that system reaches the zenith of power. And what
has happened in New Jersey in 1972 suggests that, at long last, there
has been a change in attitude toward public figures who betray a public trust. Lincoln Steffens' theory that the system, not the man, should
be held accountable—and so no individual should be severely
punished—has been rejected in the most remarkable prosecutions of
political bosses anywhere in the nation.

Other political machines have drawn larger headlines and im-
pinged to a greater degree upon public consciousness. Huey Long, for
a brief span of years, imposed a virtual dictatorship on the state of
Louisiana in the 1930s. New York's Tammany Hall, ever since the
days of Boss Tweed, has stood in the public mind as the supreme
symbol of bossism and corruption. Chicago's powerful mayor, Richard J. Daley, has been a pivotal figure in Democratic national politics
for at least two decades. Yet, search where one will, one cannot find

another political machine that has endured so long and wielded such state-wide influence as the Democratic organization of Hudson County in northern New Jersey.

Tall, angular Frank Hague, who did not exaggerate when he boasted, "I am the law," founded the system and ruled it with an iron hand for more than thirty years. He was succeeded in 1949 by John V. Kenny, known as the "Little Man," who came to power preaching reform—and then ruled in the same domineering manner as Hague, presiding over a cesspool of corruption.

The power base for this political boss system that perpetuated itself for so long was Jersey City, a grimy industrial burg directly across the Hudson River from downtown Manhattan. It is the second largest city in New Jersey, with a population of some 260,000, and it dominates the political life of Hudson County, which includes such other cities as Hoboken, Bayonne, and Weehawken. Here Frank Hague organized a political juggernaut that crushed all opposition. The huge super-patriotic parade with waving flags and banners, the martial music of marching bands, super-heated oratory that exalted Americanism and pictured the Hague machine as the savior from a Communist menace that was non-existent in predominantly Catholic Hudson County, the pressuring of the press and the smothering of all dissent—Hague plucked every string on the harpsichord of demagoguery as he whipped up the kind of mass hysteria that turned voters into robots. He determined the fate of gubernatorial aspirants, both Republican and Democratic; he sent puppets to the U.S. Senate; he decided how many names on how many gravestones would have to be voted how often to carry New Jersey for Democratic Presidential candidates.

The late Norman Thomas, the veteran Socialist leader who became quite a respected elder statesman before his death, once remarked that Jersey City "is a mirror in which other cities may see what they may become." And Professor David Dayton McKean, who compiled the most thorough study of the Hague regime in his book, *The Boss,* wrote:

". . . No awakening of civic consciousness can take place . . . against a political group which, like the one in Jersey City, controls newspapers and buys off or intimidates opposition leaders. When no effective opposition can be organized, the normal reaction to political corruption is frustrated, and a political machine can go to any length it may desire. . . . Many political machines flourish . . . and have flourished in America, but none has approached the perfection of the Hague organization in the completeness of its control over the society in which it exists. . . ."

New Jersey is a state pinched between two mighty neighbors, New York and Pennsylvania. James Madison, often called the Father of the Constitution, described it as resembling a beer keg tapped at both ends, on the north by New York City and on the south by Philadelphia. The effect on this tapped-keg of a state has been to drain away its most capable native sons, lured as they are by the greater opportunities offered by the metropolises at either extremity. It has been said that all New Jersey ever gets in return are scoundrels fleeing one step ahead of the law. Rogues who have plundered Wall Street and gangsters of the Mafia type have both adopted a simple and saving tactic: When home waters get too hot, they flee across the Delaware or the Hudson and seek refuge in the so-called Garden State, where, as yet, they have committed no unpardonable crimes and where their money buys them at least temporary immunity.

As far back as 1868, three Wall Street wheelers and dealers who had robbed the Erie Railroad blind—Daniel Drew, Jim Fisk, and Jay Gould—hopped aboard a Hudson River ferry, with process servers figuratively snapping at their coattails, and holed up with their money sacks in Taylor's Hotel in Jersey City. They surrounded themselves with an armed guard of porters, detectives, and thugs, transforming the hotel into "Fort Taylor" and defying New York authorities to touch them.

Such shady adventurers corrupted everything they touched; and it was into this climate of corruption that Frank Hague was born on January 17, 1876. His birthplace was in a house on Tenth Street in an odiferous slum known as the Horseshoe. Much of Jersey City had been originally marshland. In 1863 the Central Railroad of New Jersey, reaching out for a ferry connection with New York, extended its lines along the South Cove to the bay front. The roadbed was built over a fill composed of New York City garbage and refuse dumped from scows, and for years the stink wafted over the southern portions of Jersey City where Frank Hague was born.

His parents were both Irish, and the Horseshoe was then an almost all-Irish slum. Its residents were recent immigrants, struggling for a living and a foothold in the new world. The men worked for the railroads or the Colgate Soap Company or the Lorillard Tobacco Company. The going wage for unskilled laborers was $1 a day, and for the skilled, $1.75. Out of such wages the Irish supported some forty saloons in the Horseshoe; and when their spirits had been properly fortified by visits to such establishments, they became belligerent and engaged in innumerable brawls.

Frank Hague was the third son of John and Margaret (Fagen) Hague, who had eight children. The father, after laboring as a black-smith in the yards of the Erie Railroad, finally got himself appointed a bank guard through the influence of the local Democratic leader. It was, perhaps, Frank Hague's first lesson about the manner in which one went about improving one's situation in life.

Young Frank and his brothers lived the typical street life of boys brought up in a slum. Two of his brothers became members of a street gang bearing the ferocious name "Red Tigers," and Frank early found the life of the street far more fascinating than the drudgery of school. Indeed, it is doubtful whether any American boss wielding comparable power was ever so poorly educated. Hague himself in later years liked to describe his first day in school. He stayed for just ten minutes, then climbed out a basement window and ran away. "I was," he once said, "what folks call a bad boy. I was a truant from school, not once but many times." The result: He got only as far as the sixth grade, and in 1889, when he was thirteen, an age at which a normal student would be entering high school, he was expelled as incorrigible.

He became a drifter. If there was anything Frank Hague hated worse than school, it was work. He roamed the streets with his friends, went to dances, swam in the river, boxed. But work was not for him. He was a tall, thin boy, with long legs. His hair was reddish brown. He had a high forehead and pale blue eyes, and he spoke with an Irish accent that never left him. He seems to have had several minor brushes with the law, but he always managed to avoid serious trouble.

He spent most of his time at a local gymnasium, where he became handy with his fists. He was mixed up in a number of those street brawls that were almost daily occurrences in the Horseshoe; but he was shrewd enough to leave the dangerous fighting to others, and by the time police arrived, his long legs had always taken him out of sight.

His father tried to get him off the streets by finding him a job as a blacksmith's helper in the Erie Railroad yards, but Frank, as he said years later, did not like being "nursemaid to locomotives." He quit to become the manager of a run-of-the-mill lightweight prizefigher, Joe Craig, of Brooklyn. Craig never amounted to much, but Hague as his manager began to hang around the Cable Athletic Club and the Greenwood Social Club. It was a heady atmosphere for a boy from the Horseshoe, and Frank Hague, with his take from Joe Craig's brawling, began to play up to it, blossoming out in fine clothes. Where previously he had been clad in the hand-me-downs from his older brothers, he now appeared in four-button, double-breasted plaid suits, with a long draped cape thrown over his left shoulder. His new sartorial splendor impressed the slum dwellers of the Horseshoe.

Frank Hague, like many Irishmen, had a natural instinct for politics; and in his case, as in many others, politics offered the quickest and easiest route up out of the slums. In 1897, when he was twenty-one, the first, faint opportunity came knocking at his door. Nat Kenny, proprietor of one of the most prosperous saloons in the Horseshoe, had fallen out with the ward boss, and he needed a candidate to run for the lowly office of constable. Since no one appeared eager to buck the organization, he finally approached Hague. Hague was willing, but he needed money.

"I'll run, Mr. Kenny," he said, "but I'll need some money. I ain't got a dime."

"How much will you need?" Kenny asked.

"Well, about $75, if I'm to make friends."

Kenny handed over the $75, and Frank Hague's political career was launched. He was elected constable, a position that paid no salary but gave him fees for whatever services he might perform. The position, on the very lowest rung of the political ladder, had for Hague, however, a certain importance: It enabled him to mingle with some of the politicians of the city. And he mingled so well that, in just two years, he was attached to the sheriff's office as a deputy at a salary of $25 a week.

Frank Hague was now on his way. In 1903 he married Jenny Warner, a girl from the Horseshoe, and he constantly expanded his circle of acquaintances. In October, 1904, however, there occurred an incident that might have finished the career of a lesser man. An old friend from street-gang days, Thomas (Red) Dugan, had become a burglar, confidence man, pickpocket, ballot-stuffer, and thug. He had served four years in prison for bouncing a bullet off the skull of a pastor's wife in an attempted burglary; and in the fall of 1904, he was arrested in Boston for palming off a forged certified check on a bank and defrauding the institution of $500. Frank Hague and another deputy sheriff went up to Boston and tried to establish an alibi for Red Dugan, arguing they had seen him in Jersey City at the time he was supposed to have been passing the phony check in Boston. Their testimony wasn't very effective, and they failed to save Red Dugan. But Hague, at least, got himself into a lot of trouble. He was supposed to have been appearing as a witness before a grand jury on the day he went to Boston. Judge John A. Blair was incensed, hauled Hague up before him on a contempt of court charge and gave him a tongue-lashing. He also fined the future boss $100 and discharged him from further service as an officer of the court.

In respectable circles, the disgrace attending such a misadventure might have been expected to end a man's career, but in the Horseshoe the only effect was to make Frank Hague something of a hero. The word was spread around that he gone up to Boston in an attempt to save Red Dugan only because Red's mother had pleaded with him so tearfully. It was an explanation that appealed to the sentimental streak in many voters, and Hague's constituents within two years made him boss of the Second Ward.

The city-wide boss at this time was Robert Davis, and Hague, having lost his deputy sheriff's post, appealed to Davis to do something for him. Davis did. In December, 1906, Davis' Democratic machine designated Hague sergeant-at-arms for the state Assembly in Trenton. Although Hague owed his appointment to Davis, this did not guarantee his loyalty. In the jungle game of Jersey City politics, one didn't hesitate to bite the hand of a benefactor if there was something to be gained by the biting. Hague had a hunch that the rising power in the city was H. Otto Wittpenn, a reform mayor who was opposing Davis, and in 1908 he joined forces with Wittpenn, accepting from the mayor an appointment as City Hall custodian, a kind of glorified chief janitor.

The job paid $2,000 a year, the most Hague had ever earned, but the money was less important than the new contacts Hague made in City Hall. The young men with whom he now associated were to become the future pillars of his organization.

The most important was A. Harry Moore, Mayor Wittpenn's secretary. Moore was 29 at the time, handsome and charming, already a talented public speaker capable of delivering the telling anecdote and impressing a crowd. He was a Presbyterian and taught a Sunday School class; he belonged to the Masons; he belonged to almost every civic group of any importance. Here, Hague saw, was the ideal political candidate.

Equally important, but on a different plane, was the second friendship that Hague formed. This was with John Milton, a young lawyer in the corporation counsel's office. Milton possessed one of the shrewdest legal brains in New Jersey. He lacked Moore's flair; he did not have the qualities that make a good political campaigner. But he was a wise advisor, an ideal behind-the-scenes man. In time he was to become known as the most influential brain in the Hague machine.

To these two new friends Hague added an old one. When he became City Hall custodian, he had it in his power to name a number of deputies, and he gave one of these posts to an old street friend from the Horseshoe, chubby John Malone. Malone was to become in time Hague's deputy mayor—and the voice of Hague himself when the boss was absent from the city, as he often was.

These were the three, then—Moore, Milton, and Malone—who were to become the principal cogs in the Hague machine. Milton and Hague formed the first alliance. Milton did not like Wittpenn and resigned. Hague and Milton then conspired on the next step to be taken, the election of Hague as street and water commissioner in 1911. With this victory, Hague cut loose from Wittpenn, taking no more orders from City Hall. About the same time, Boss Davis died, and the Democratic leadership in the city was up for grabs. Hague intended to grab it.

He and John Milton put their canny heads together and decided that a reform movement that was highly popular at the time might just be ideal for their purposes. Reformers all over the nation were advocating a new type of municipal government—city commissions, with each commissioner having a designated role, to replace large and unwieldly city councils. The theory was that the commission form of government would fix responsibility and be far more efficient. But Hague and Milton took a different view. They saw that it would be easier to control a five-man commission than a large city council.

With this object in mind, Hague suddenly began to act like the most zealous of reformers. He denounced the council form of government as a breeder of "cheap politics," the instrument of "the professional politician." No one seemed to ask the obvious question: What was Frank Hague himself if not a professional politician? The reformers, innocent of the Byzantine ways of politics, as they so often are, embraced this new recruit to the cause of good government, and in the municipal election of April 15, 1913, Harry Moore and Hague were elected to fill two of the five posts on the new city commission. The commission named Mark Fagan mayor, Moore commissioner of parks and public buildings, and Hague director of public safety—a post that gave him control over the police and fire departments.

The dictatorial streak in Hague became at once apparent. He appears to have realized that he who controls the police controls in large measure the machinery of the state. And so, between 1913 and 1917, Frank Hague swept out the Jersey City Police Department and refashioned it to suit his own purposes.

His public explanation for his wholesale housecleaning (he put as many as 225 men on trial in a single day for violation of departmental rules) was that the force had been badly corrupted. No doubt it had been; Jersey City was a badly corrupted municipality. But purification was not Frank Hague's real purpose. It was simply a smokescreen that enabled him to garner headlines as he dismissed hundreds of policemen, broke sergeants and captains back to pounding beats, levied heavy fines on men who were not dismissed—and then filled the gaps in the ranks with his own hand-picked followers. He also instituted a spy system. He formed a corps of undercover men who reported directly to him about any grumbling in the ranks. It was the beginning of a covert reign of terror that, in the end, would establish Frank Hague as "the law."

The city election of 1917 was crucial for Hague. To make his power complete, he needed to seize control of the entire city commission. Mayor Fagan had made an enviable record. He had reduced the city budget and the tax rate; he had increased the assessments on the properties of huge corporations that had not been bearing anywhere near their proper share of the tax burden. Moreover, Lincoln Steffens thought highly of him and lauded him in one of his magazine articles on city government. But Frank Hague, thirsting for supreme power, was determined to bring Fagan down; and so he and A. Harry Moore headed a ticket that was designated, ironically, "the Unbossed."

Hague and Moore made huge political capital out of the fact that Mayor Fagan had brought outside experts into Jersey City to help with his reforms. What about the home-grown talent, they asked, appealing to the lowest form of local prejudice. Wasn't Jersey City capable of handling its own affairs? They also made the most of a second, low-level but telling issue. Fagan had started a $3 million school-building program that could be financed without new taxes, thanks to the economies he had effected. But the new public school program got under way just at a time when the Catholic Church was planning to build a number of parochial schools. Hague, whose Catholicism was as total as his distaste for education was profound, denounced the public school expenditures, playing up to the lowest religious prejudices of his constituency.

These two issues were enough to topple the honorable and conscientious Mayor Fagan. When the votes were counted, all five members of Hague's "unbossed" ticket had been swept into office. On May 15, 1917, the new "unbossed" commission met and named Frank Hague the mayor of Jersey City. The long reign had begun.

Hague's first act as the new, all-powerful boss was to pad the public payroll. Key supporters were given their just rewards and began to feed at the municipal trough. The budget, cut by Fagan, now began to zoom. Taxes had to be raised to meet the increased costs of Hague's greedy machine, but naturally Hague himself did not want to antagonize the average man, whose vote was so important, by raising his taxes. Thus he boosted the assessments of big corporations. Nine major railroads had tracks, sidings, and terminals in Jersey City at the time, and their property had been assessed at an average of $3,000 an acre compared to $17,000 an acre for other real estate. Hague hit them hard, raising total assesments from $67 million to $160 million. He also boosted the assessments of Standard Oil Company of New Jersey from $1.5 million to $14 million, and those of the Public Service Corporation from $3 million to $30 million.

These were huge increases, and the corporations screamed as only mighty corporations can. They appealed the assessments to the State Board of Taxes and Assessments in Trenton, and the board obligingly threw out the new tax levies. This action put Hague in a bind. He had to have the additional revenue; moreover, he had to get it without soaking the great mass of voters. There was only one solution—he would have to elect a handpicked governor who would have the power to pack the state tax board with new appointees willing to do Frank Hague's bidding.

The new boss had little difficulty in finding the right puppet. His man was Edward I. Edwards, then a state senator from Hudson County—a banker, a Protestant, a Moose, a Mason, an Eagle, a member of almost any and every organization that might help a politician to get votes.

Edwards' rival for the Democratic nomination was James R. Nugent, the boss of Newark, New Jersey's largest city and the seat of populous Essex County. Nugent had been considered the state Democratic leader ever since Woodrow Wilson had left New Jersey to become President in 1913, and the gubernatorial contest of 1919 was considered a showdown that would determine party control for a long time. Hague won the test, piling up a margin of 22,000 votes for Edwards in Hudson County, more than enough to offset Nugent's 13,000 lead in Essex County. In the general election in November, Hague's Hudson machine did even better. It piled up 58,527 votes for Edwards to 23,000 for his Republican opponent. Thus Hague had his first governor.

Now began a process that was to continue for decades in New Jersey. Governor Edwards ousted the members of the state highway commission and appointed Hague men to fill the vacancies. Using the governor's power of appointment, he packed state boards, commissions, and courts with obliging men who would do the boss's bidding. The state Attorney General, the principal law-enforcing officer, was inevitably a Hague creature; so, too, were the prosecutors in many counties. As Hague governor succeeded Hague governor, the appointive power was used to pack some eighty state boards and agencies either with Hague Democrats or with hybrid personalities known as Hague Republicans. The most disastrous effect of this on-going process was the eventual corruption of the judicial machinery of New Jersey. With the Attorney General and prosecutors subservient to Hague, with complaisant judges ready to protect him from attack in the courts, the boss became invulnerable to investigation and prosecution—no matter what he did.

Hague could not have accomplished this miracle of immunity without the cooperation of his supposed political enemies, the Republicans. The rural counties of New Jersey were dominated, almost without exception, by Republican bosses and their machines, kindred

operators who were just as powerful and ruthless in their smaller baili-
wicks as Hague was in Hudson County. In state-wide contests, Hague
could elect governors because he could phony the election returns in
Hudson County to suit his need; but the Republican county machines always controlled the legislature. Since Republican state senators had
to approve the appointments of prosecutors and judges in their counties, this meant that boss had to deal with boss and that prosecutors
and judges, to get their posts, had to be willing to serve two masters.

In this fashion, a pernicious practice developed by which Hague
and the affected Republican bosses sought to ensure this servitude.
Appointees, if there existed any doubt about their loyalty, were required to sign blank resignations before they got their jobs. One copy
went into the safe of the Republican boss, the other into Frank
Hague's office in Jersey City. Anytime a prosecutor or a judge failed
to perform as instructed in matters vital to either boss, all the of-
fended boss had to do was to type in the date on that blank resigna-
tion and mail it to the office of the Secretary of State. In some instances, distinguished officials who had resigned for reasons of "ill
health," the usual stated cause, were so dumbfounded they could
hardly conceal their surprise when newspaper reporters telephoned
them the news that they were out.

New Jersey became virtually prostrate under this dual boss system which served the political purposes of the machines of both parties, regardless of the public welfare. When Edward I. Edwards' term
as governor expired, Hague sent him on to Washington as a U.S. Senator and got George S. Silzer elected to succeed him in Trenton. Silzer,
in turn, was followed in the election of 1925 by Hague's favorite and
perennial candidate, the handsome A. Harry Moore. By this time,
Hague's control over the Democratic machinery was so complete that
there was no opposition to Moore. *The New York Times* reported:
"He [Moore] can talk circles around any other politician in New Jersey. He has joined every social organization that is helpful to a candidate. . . . There is nothing of interest to the average citizen that he
can't 'orate' about with the facility of a river flowing over a dam."

New Jersey governors at that time could not succeed themselves,
but periodically over the years, whenever Hague desperately needed a
governor, he pulled A. Harry Moore out of his hat like a magician
producing a white rabbit. Three times this happened, and three times
Moore was elected governor. Whenever he ran, it was noteworthy that

many Republican bosses in the rural counties gave only a faintly murmured lip-service to the candidate of their own party. "Harry Moore is a fine man," their underlings would say, with a knowing smirk; and when the votes were counted, it would turn out that perhaps Moore hadn't quite carried these Republican strongholds, but in many he had achieved a virtual standoff—a mysterious display of strength that made him a landslide winner when the cataract of Democratic votes rushed in from Hudson County.

The fraudulent nature of such floodtides remained a public scandal in New Jersey for years. Moore won his first gubernatorial contest by 38,000 votes, thanks to a whopping 103,000 plurality in Hudson County. The Republicans, not quite so well-trained in the intricacies of the dual boss system as they later became, challenged the legitimacy of these returns. Thomas McDonald, a Republican, then the superintendent of the Hudson County Board of Elections, pinpointed the frauds. Many persons had voted, giving addresses that turned out to be vacant lots. In one polling place, the impossible had happened: Moore's Republican opponent hadn't been credited with a single vote, though some voters claimed they had voted for him. In some instances, the number of votes counted exceeded the number of registered voters; in one district where there were only 662 names in the poll book, 683 votes had been tallied. All of these charges were turned over to the Hudson County prosecutor for investigation. But who was the prosecutor? It was none other than John Milton, Hague's private brain truster. Milton brushed off the charges like a man shooing a fly. They were grossly exaggerated, he said, and besides, the grand jury had its hands full of more important matters. And that was that.

The manner in which the courts similarly protected Hague when protests got beyond the prosecutor's level was illustrated in a number of cases. The career of Thomas J. Brogan, who became Chief Justice of the New Jersey Supreme Court thanks to Governor Moore, demonstrated how this protective system worked. Brogan had attended the College of Saint Francis Xavier and Fordham Law School. Admitted to the bar in 1912, he had become active in Jersey City politics. Hague had made him corporation counsel in 1921, and he had held that post for eleven years. In 1932 Governor Moore appointed him an associate justice of the Supreme Court, and when the incumbent chief justice died shortly afterward, Moore elevated Brogan to fill the vacancy.

Brogan's subsequent ruling in Jersey City election cases defied rational explanation. In a city election held in 1933, a number of residents in one district filed affidavits with the superintendent of elections, contending they had voted for an anti-organization candidate who had not been credited with a single vote. Chief Justice Brogan ruled that the superintendent of elections had no right to open the ballot boxes in an effort to determine what had happened. The court, he acknowledged, had the power, but he refused to exercise it. The Supreme Court upheld this ruling by its chief justice. In a similar case in 1937, Brogan's reasoning was even more bewildering. He had the right to order the ballot boxes opened, he said, but no one had the right to look inside. Therefore, there was no sense in opening the boxes; case dismissed.

Such brazen rulings demonstrated Hague's ironclad control over the courts. They also served to protect the boss on another level— when he was personally attacked as the major beneficiary of his corrupted regime. The mayor never earned more than $8,000 a year legitimately, but he rapidly accumulated a fortune that eventually ran into millions of dollars. On one occasion in 1929, when the hopelessness of trying to expose Hague was less obvious than it later became, some Republican mavericks in the state legislature initiated an investigation of Hudson County. Thereupon, the so-called Case Committee was formed, which probed deeply into the maze of financial dealings that had made Mayor Hague an exceedingly wealthy man.

Specifically, it discovered that the mayor had adopted the practice of buying up parcels of costly real estate, using a technique that never varied. The purchases would be made by a front man, a "dummy," whom Hague would later reimburse in cash. With John Milton fronting for him in this fashion, he had purchased the site on which the Duncan Hall apartment house was built in Jersey City. Milton paid $51,000 by check; Hague returned the money to him in cash. With Milton again fronting for him, the mayor purchased an expensive summer house in the exclusive seaside community of Deal, New Jersey. The cost was $65,000, and Hague again gave Milton the cash. The Case Committee, totaling these and other transactions, reported that, largely between 1921 and 1929, the $8,000-a-year mayor had invested a total of $392,910.50, all in cash passed along to his dummy representatives.

Where had it come from? The committee believed it had found some answers. It reported that the improvement of Journal Square in Jersey City had cost $1,643,574.87—but the city had paid out $3,162,021.42. A New York resident, H. S. Kerbaugh, seemed to have had an uncanny knack of acquiring tracts of land that Jersey City was about to condemn at greatly inflated prices. Three such deals between 1919 and 1924 had resulted in a mysterious profit of $628,145, and the committee concluded that such phenomenal success in land speculation could have resulted only from "a conspiracy operating under cover of legal forms."

Naturally, the committee sought to get Mayor Hague to explain these mysteries, but the mayor was flatly contemptuous. The following question-and-answer sequence, taken from the committee record, is typical:

Q. Did Mr. Milton purchase for your account the remainder of the land on which Duncan Hall stands and pay for it $51,000?

A. I decline to answer.

Q. Did you reimburse him in cash for $51,000?

A. I decline to answer.

Q. If you reimbursed him to the extent of $51,000 in cash, why did you handle the business in that way?

A. I decline to answer.

Q. Was there any reason for making a cash payment, the payment not being made by check?

A. I refuse to answer.

The average citizen who dared to defy a legislative committee in this fashion would doubtless wind up in jail—but not Frank Hague. The Case Committee had the boss brought before a session of the whole legislature, but he simply repeated the refrain: "I decline to answer." He was then arrested for contempt, but Hague by now could count on the courts. Vice Chancellor John J. Fallon, who had been a Hudson County counsel and assemblyman, freed him on a writ of habeas corpus, contending the legislature had no right to question Hague because it was usurping judicial functions in attempting to show a criminal conspiracy. The Case Committee appealed to the Court of Errors and Appeals, the state's highest tribunal, but this court divided evenly, six to six—and so, in effect, upheld the ruling of the vice chancellor.

"I am very much pleased and satisfied with the decision," Hague told the press. "It is exactly what I expected."

The court ruling virtually killed off the Case Committee; it never did get the answers to the questions it had raised.

Such episodes, repeated time and again, demonstrated the total authority and immunity of Frank Hague. If anything more was needed to make the shame of New Jersey complete, Hague supplied it in 1939 when he had his unqualified son, Frank Hague, Jr., named to the Court of Errors and Appeals. Governor Moore, in office again, performed the deed on February 20, 1939. He was naming young Hague a lay judge of the court, Moore said, because he knew the appointment would "make his daddy happy."

If New Jersey residents did not retch at this flagrant statement, they should have, for Frank Hague, Jr. had just one thing to recommend him—he was the boss's son. Professor McKean later described the young man's credentials in these words:

"He was . . . like his father almost impervious to education, in spite of the most expensive private schools and tutors. He attended the Kingsley School, the Princeton Preparatory School, and the Milford School. This battery at length got him into Princeton in 1927. At the end of his first year he had to go to summer school to repeat the courses he had failed." Even summer school could not bring young Hague abreast of his class, and he left Princeton in 1930 "to study elsewhere." The "elsewhere" turned out to be the University of Virginia Law School. "His stay at Virginia was notable in two ways: he married Mary Katherine Jordon, daughter of a dean, and he failed nine of the twenty courses he took in law school," Professor McKean wrote. A transfer to Washington and Lee did not help. "He studied, off and on, until 1936, when he gave up. He was never graduated. Unable to obtain a law degree, he nevertheless attempted the same year that he left Washington and Lee the New Jersey bar examination, which two-thirds of the candidates normally fail on their first attempt. But he passed."

He served his clerkship in the most congenial law office imaginable—that of John Milton. But at the time of his appointment, there was no record that he had ever tried a case.

The designation of the intellectually barren Frank Hague, Jr. to the state's highest court shocked many of New Jersey's most distinguished lawyers, but the bulk of the legal profession surrendered supinely to the inevitable. The Hudson County Bar Association almost did handsprings. Five hundred members signed a petition backing young Hague, no doubt making "his daddy happy." Louis Marciante, president of the State Federation of Labor, chipped in with an endorsement in which he charged that opposition came only from "radicals" and from "the dying [and rival] Congress of Industrial Organizations." More important, on the level of practical politics, was the support of the so-called Hague Republicans. This was a faction headed by Harold G. Hoffman, who was to be twice elected governor with tacit Hague support—"That little fellow, he's a million," Hague once said admiringly, and when Hoffman ran, it was remarkable how few names on the gravestones rose to register their votes in Hudson County. With such a bipartisan, mutual-admiration society operating, it was perhaps not surprising that six Hoffman-Hague Republicans in the state Senate joined with seven Hague Democrats in voting for confirmation, and Frank Hague, Jr. took his seat on the court. Summing up, the *New Jersey Law Journal* commented that "it is not altogether a matter of hindsight to say that the confirmation of this appointment was a foregone conclusion. Perhaps the bar did not wish to tilt with a windmill. Perhaps there were fears of reprisals, judicial and political. . . . Nevertheless, whatever the reason, lawyers as a group have suffered another blow, rightly or wrongly."

The boss who could silence all opposition and crush an entire state under his heel became by a natural political process a major figure on the national scene. After 1920, even when the organization was not yet the smoothly functioning machine it later became, no Democratic Pesidential candidate ever failed to carry Hudson County, and every Democratic Presidential candidate had to be aware that his chances of victory in the state depended upon the degree of his cordiality with Frank Hague. Hague headed the New Jersey delegation to the Democratic National Convention in New York in 1924, and there Jersey Democrats fought to the final ballot for the nomination of New York's Governor Alfred E. Smith. Smith and Hague had become great friends. Both had risen from the slums; both were devout Irish Catholics; both liked baseball games and prizefights. Their families visited each other, and they often relaxed on the same cruise ships together.

The Democratic convention deadlocked in 1924, denying Smith the coveted nomination, but Frank Hague came out of the long party brawl a bigger man than ever—the Vice Chairman of the Democratic National Committee, a post of honor he was to hold for decades. In the election of 1928, Hague was again in Al Smith's corner; and when Smith got the nomination, Hague's Hudson County machine functioned as never before. It rolled up 153,000 votes for Smith to 99,000 for Herbert Hoover, but the Hoover landslide was too strong for the votes stolen in Hudson to have their usual magical effect. New Jersey went for the engineer over the Happy Warrior by 925,000 to 616,000.

The disastrous Hoover administration and the onset of the Great Depression in 1929 made it clear to Smith and Hague that the Democrat who got his party's nomination in 1932 almost certainly would be elected. Smith hoped to run again, but there was a new and dangerous figure to the political horizon—Governor Franklin D. Roosevelt, of New York. Wedded to Smith by personal and political ties, Hague now committed one of his greatest political blunders: He tried to line up anti-Roosevelt delegates in the Middle Atlantic States, and he went to Chicago early to become the floor manager of the Smith forces.

He not only put himself out on a limb by these activities; he virtually sawed off the limb behind him. As vice chairman of the national committee, he might have been expected outwardly at least, to have assumed an impartial role; but he was so partisan that he went overboard, issuing a public statement in which he said that Roosevelt, "if nominated, has no chance of winning the election in November." Hague boasted that he had felt out public sentiment "in practically every state in the union," and he made the flat prediction that Roosevelt could not carry "a single state east of the Mississippi and very few in the Far West. . . ."

The statement reflected a flaw that is almost a common denominator of powerful political bosses—stupidity concerning larger issues. Even the man in the street knew at the time that Roosevelt, if nominated, had a good chance to be elected; but Frank Hague, like many bosses before and since—Mayor Daley, who helped to tear the Democratic Party apart in the savage convention in Chicago in 1968, is a prime example—had become so accustomed to wielding autocratic power that he could not conceive the public might not want what he wanted. Despite Roosevelt's huge lead in the delegate count, delusion continued to befog Hague's mind. On June 30, he crowed: "We've got them licked." Somebody was "licked" all right, but that somebody was Al Smith.

Nursing his wounds on the mournful return trip to New Jersey, the Boss was faced with a key decision. Smith was his friend, and an angry Smith had said that he would not support Roosevelt. But did Frank Hague, who had blundered so badly that he had egg all over his face, dare to take a similar stand? Suppose Roosevelt *did* carry New Jersey without him. Suppose Roosevelt *was* elected. Then where would Frank Hague be? The Boss shuddered, thinking of the dire possibilities. In such an event, he would have lost all influence in Washington; he would have nothing to say about jobs, appointments, the handling of federal money. What was worse, a hostile U.S. Attorney General could come nosing around in Hudson County, and no one knew better than Frank Hague some of the things he might find. Such a disaster must not be allowed to happen; and so no sooner had the Boss returned to Jersey City than he announced he was going to support Franklin Roosevelt all the way. That ended the long friendship between Frank Hague and Al Smith, but in politics a man has to save himself first and let his friends look out for themselves as best they can.

His decision announced, Hague telephoned James A. Farley, Roosevelt's campaign manager, and promised to stage for Roosevelt "the largest political rally ever held in the United States." Roosevelt agreed to speak on August 27 at the National Guard camp ground in Sea Girt, New Jersey; and Hague, making good on his promise to Farley, turned out his trained legions in a mass demonstration so huge it stunned all observers. "If it wasn't the biggest rally in history up to that time, it must have been very close to it," an awed Jim Farley later wrote. Buses, special trains, and a limousine fleet took at least 150,000 of the faithful to Sea Girt (Hague claimed the figure was closer to 250,000), and Roosevelt, impressed, was reported to have said that "only my old friend, Mayor Hague, could have done that."

This sudden "old friend" continued to function on election day. Hague's Hudson County organization produced a veritable tidal wave of Roosevelt votes, far surpassing what it had done for Al Smith in

1928. Roosevelt carried the Hague barony by 184,000 to 66,000, a margin that was vital to him, for he won the state by only 806,000 to 775,000. By this demonstration of power, Hague solidified his ties to the new source of power in Washington. His Congressmen and Senators were instructed to vote the White House line without question; and, knowing they would not long remain Congressmen or Senators if they disobeyed, they never failed. Roosevelt, ever the practical politician, returned favor for favor.

The New Deal broke with such corrupt political regimes as Tammany Hall in New York, where Roosevelt aided the independent fusion mayor, Fiorello H. LaGuardia; with the Pendergast machine in Kansas City; with Huey Long in Louisiana. The enormous powers of the Justice Department were thrown into Missouri and Louisiana to prosecute machines whose corruption and flouting of democratic principles had become notorious. But Jersey City and Hudson County remained immune from the attentions of the federal watchdogs. Frank Hague's gravestone votes on election day were too essential to victory in the state and the maintenance of power in Washington; and so, though many New Dealers had no love for the Hague regime, the motto in the capital became, "Clear it with Hague." The enormous sums of money poured out in new federal relief and work projects (these meant $500,000 a month to Jersey City, Hague said) were all funneled through the hands of the Hague machine. Appointments to federal courts and agencies were cleared with the Boss; no man could get a federal plum without his approval.

Thus, with no checkrein upon it, the Hague machine became ever more dictatorial. Hague mesmerized the public with great parades and rallies, held at least four times a year, with flags waving, aerial bombs exploding, and fireworks lighting up the sky. These were called "Americanization Day" parades, and the whipping boy, in a city that was 75 per cent Catholic, was always the non-existent Communist menace. "Stand shoulder to shoulder with Mayor Hague and keep the Communists out," placards proclaimed. Anyone who dissented, anyone who criticized the Hague regime, automatically became a "radical" or a "Red." Wrapping itself in the folds of the flag, the machine loosed its thugs and billy-wielding police on such troublemakers, whether they were labor organizers, civil rights advocates, or political opponents trying to check up on the chicanery at the polls on election day.

The brutality that helped to protect and perpetuate election-day frauds became notorious. On one occasion 245 students from Princeton University went to Jersey City to watch an election for the Honest Ballot Association. Within an hour of their arrival, five were beaten up so badly that they had to be taken to a hospital; others were forcibly ejected from the polling places. The students protested to Mayor Hague, who told them: "Well, you fellows can go back there [to the polling places] if you wish, but if you get knocked cold it will be your own hard luck."

In 1937 the *Jersey Journal,* which for a time opposed Hague but finally saw the hopelessness of it all and gave up, inquired caustically what was the sense of having an election superintendent and deputies to watch the polls in view of the widespread frauds. Commissioner John Ferguson replied frankly that he and his deputies were of no value because they were helpless before the nightsticks of Hague's bully-boy police. Some of his deputies, he said, "were locked up in police stations; some were stuck on corners, with a threat that if they moved from there, a nightstick would be wrapped around their necks. . . . In front of one polling place I counted two police captains in uniform, one captain in plain clothes, one Jersey City commissioner, and ten uniformed policemen. Of what earthly value were my two deputies? The police officers laughed at them, . . . told them that if they opened their mouths they would wake up in the hospital."

All of this was happening, of course, in America—the so-called "land of the free." Were Americans, then, so utterly helpless that they couldn't protest or didn't dare? In Hudson County in Hague's time, the answer had to be "Yes."

Hague bought, bribed, or intimidated until all opposition was crushed. He constantly swelled the ranks of his political army by padding the public payroll, paying off with jobs those who paid off for him. For years Jersey City had two "cuspidor cleaners" at $1950 a year apiece, and a "foreman of vacuum cleaners" at $4000. A "street laborer" who acknowledged that his only task was to pick up whatever boxes might fall off a truck in a two-block area drew $1700 a year. The Democratic leader of the Ninth District of the Third Ward, a man who tended bar in his own saloon every day, was also listed as a laborer in a bathhouse at $2200 annually.

Those who held such good-pay, no-show jobs naturally were in no position to protest when Hague levied special assessments upon them. All officeholders were compelled to kick in 3 per cent of their annual salaries to the organization's political kitty, filling John Malone's safe in City Hall with as many greenbacks as one might find in a bank vault. But this was not all. Extra assessments were sometimes levied to help the Catholic Church, the one force that might effectively have opposed Hague. When the church needed extra money for building improvements or a new parochial school, Hague expected his followers to kick in another 3 per cent of their salaries. The church was also taken care of in other ways. Some of its priests were on the public payroll; almost all of the important offices in city government were filled by Catholics; and Hague posed, as the great protector against the "Red menace." The result was that the church remained throughout his regime his faithful ally.

Catholics were not alone in succumbing to the tactics that silenced potentially dangerous religious critics. Protestants and Jews were equally susceptible to Hague's mightiest weapon, the public job that was, in effect, a bribe. During the hard times of the 1930s, the city and county paid twelve chaplains $20,900 annually for their part-time services. Professor McKean explained some of the miracles wrought by such payments, writing:

". . . A few years ago one preacher gave a series of sermons against the Hague administration; returning from Europe, he announced to reporters that he had seen no city on his travels the streets of which were so dirty and littered. He is now a chaplain and no longer sees anything to criticize. . . . One preacher who started a campaign against the machine, and offered prayers every Sunday for the deliverance of Jersey City from the hands of the rapacious politicians, lost interest when his daughter was given a job at City Hall. . . . Other preachers and priests have been listed as 'utility men' on the payroll, and one was even called a plumber's helper."

Such wholesale padding of the public payroll sent the Jersey City budget into the stratosphere and gave the city the highest tax rate in the nation. Businesses threatened to leave, and Hague, to prevent this disaster, offered them the only compensation in his power: He embarked on a career of union-busting that made Jersey City an 80 per cent "open shop" town, with wages lower than were being paid for comparable jobs elsewhere.

Nevertheless, some important businessmen were unhappy; some felt that conditions in Jersey City were simply intolerable—and something ought to be done. One such business group got Mayor Hague to meet with it. Spokesmen recited a long list of complaints: high taxes, inefficient government, poor public schools. Then they asked Hague what he intended to do. According to Professor McKean: "He arose and told each man what favors he had received from the organization, what laws he was violating or had violated, or what money he owed to banks of which the Mayor was a stockholder or director. He reminded others of the relatives they had on the public payroll, and he told some of them of business practices in which they had engaged that would not make good publicity. Then he put on his hat and walked out. . . ."

The autocratic and brutal qualities of the Hague regime became more and more apparent with the years. Stubborn political opponents who could not be bribed or intimidated were simply beaten up by Hague's police. Jefferson Burkitt and James Cullom, two stubborn critics, were bludgeoned so often that their trips to the hospital ceased to be news. On one occasion, as Burkitt alighted from a bus to attend a meeting, he was seized by police, taken into the basement of the courthouse, and beaten so savagely that he had to be held upright when he was brought before a judge the next morning. Then he was sentenced to ninety days in jail on a trumped-up charge that he had used abusive language to a policeman.

Labor organizers were also arrested, harassed, brutally treated. Hague's police broke up every strike attempted in Jersey City from 1931 to 1937. Then came the great confrontation with the Congress of Industrial Organizations (CIO), the new and militant labor union that had begun competing with the older American Federation of Labor. When the CIO attempted to come into Jersey City, its organizers were arrested, their leaflets confiscated, meeting halls barred to them. The American Civil Liberties Union entered the dispute, applying for a permit to hold an open-air meeting to discuss civil rights under the Constitution. Hague, in his favorite role of protecting his turf against radicals and Reds, ordered his underlings to reject the request, and the CIO and ACLU went to court.

It was just at this time, in November of 1937, that Hague uttered his most famous line. He had bragged in one radio speech, murdering English grammar in his customary fashion, that "Jersey City is the most moralest city in America." He often boasted, with truth, that there were no cheap dance halls or houses of prostitution in Jersey City, but he never attempted to explain why such places clustered just over the city line in the Hudson County that he dominated. In line with his "most moralest" theme, he was especially proud of his program to curb juvenile delinquency. This consisted of giving his police complete authority to handle young troublemakers, shunning the usual court processes. In a speech on November 10, 1937, he described an incident in which he had played a personal role. Two boys, both under sixteen, had been arrested for truancy, he said, and he had suggested that jobs be found for them to keep them out of trouble. He was told that this couldn't be done because the New Jersey Working Papers Law forbade the employment of such young children. At this, Hague exploded. He quoted himself as saying: "Listen, here is the law! I am the law!"

The timing of this declaration, coming as it did just when Hague was embroiled in his great confrontation with the CIO, made huge headlines across the nation. The Boss was much aggrieved. He felt that his words had been given an importance far beyond what was justified; but later, when he was called as a witness in the CIO-civil liberties trial, he in effect repeated them. At one point, jabbing a forefinger at his chest, he exclaimed: "I decide. I do. Me." He was then asked whether his "I am the law" statement was "to all practical intents and purposes true." And Hague replied: "Yes."

When he was asked whether he believed in such civil rights as freedom of speech and assembly, as guaranteed by the Constitution, he replied in tangled syntax: "Whenever I hear a discussion of civil rights and the rights of free speech and the rights of the Constitution, always remember you will find him with a Russian flag under his coat; you never miss." It can be said with certainty that the Founding Fathers of this republic, perhaps the greatest generation of men we have ever produced, would have been profoundly shocked at such a statement, betraying as it did what they considered one of their most sacred principles, one that was the very cornerstone of freedom.

In the end, the CIO trial was damaging to Hague. He was compelled to admit that his anti-labor campaign, despite its offer of cheap wages, had not lured major businesses to Jersey City. All it had brought were sweatshops. *Life* published photographs showing one family of four, including a child kept out of school, hard at work in their home making lampshades. The wages for *all four came to just $2.50 a day!* Such were the human costs of the Hague regime.

Hague's flouting of the Constitution was too much for the courts to swallow. He lost the CIO case in the Federal District Court in Newark, appealed the decision all the way up to the U.S. Supreme Court—and lost all the way. Subsequently, a truce of sorts was arranged between the CIO and City Hall. Hague could no longer afford the roughhouse tactics he had previously employed to keep the CIO from organizing, but he wrung from CIO leaders a denunciation of the national leadership of the Republican Party and a pledge to support Democrats. In Hudson, of course, this meant supporting Hague.

The result was that Hague remained supreme through the decade of the 1940s. He was still boss in Hudson County; he was still Vice Chairman of the Democratic National Committee; he still had the power to determine the outcome of state elections. He retired a bit into the background, leaving the mechanics of running City Hall to his nephew, Frank Hague Eggers, as mayor; but in all that mattered, he was still the Boss. Then came 1948 and a repetition of the blunder of 1932.

Harry S. Truman had succeeded President Roosevelt in the White House. Naturally, he expected to be his party's standard bearer, but many politicians felt that he could not be elected, that the party needed a stronger candidate. A week before the party convention was to meet, Hague made his move. He summoned New Jersey Democrats to a meeting on the morning of July 4 in the Berkeley-Carteret Hotel in Asbury Park. There he tossed a bombshell. His choice for the Presidential nomination, he announced, was General of the Army Dwight D. Eisenhower.

A politician as astute as Hague supposedly was might have been expected to have ascertained in advance, before he put his own neck on the line, that his prospective candidate was willing. It quickly became clear that Hague had not bothered to take this elementary precaution, for General Eisenhower promptly announced that, under no conditions, would he be a candidate. The move to dump Truman collapsed, and once more Frank Hague found himself out on the end of a very long and sagging limb.

As he had in 1932, he attempted to save himself by staging a rally so huge that President Truman would realize he had to have the support of Frank Hague in New Jersey. The event was scheduled for

Jersey City on October 7, 1948. Louis A. Lepis, a mathematics teacher and former high school football coach, then serving as Director of the Jersey City Recreation Department, later recalled what happened on that historic night. Lepis' job was to combine two marching bands of the recreation department into one huge ensemble to lead the parade.

"As I approached the starting point," Lepis later wrote, "the surrounding streets were already jammed with thousands of the party faithful, lined up by 'wards,' and holding small American flags. It was a typical Hague-ordered, command performance."

Hague had decreed that this was to be the largest, most colorful parade ever staged in Jersey City, but Lepis soon sensed that something was decidedly wrong. Police Commissioner Dan Casey told him the Boss wanted to see him down a side street. There Lepis found Hague in a distraught state. "He stammered and stuttered as he spoke to me—so much so that I impulsively laid my hand on his arm to calm him," Lepis wrote. He was astonished to find Hague on the street handling details that ordinarily would be left to an underling, and equally astonished at the nature of the problem that so exercised the Boss. It was simply this: Hague wanted one of those recreation department bands taken from the head of the parade and brought down to lead a group of women marching under the banner, "Housewives for Truman." The stammering and stuttering, Hague's obvious agitation over such a minor detail, forced Lepis to conclude: "The Boss was really gone."

Afterwards, he learned what had happened. There had been a reception for the Trumans before the parade. Truman had passed through the crowd, shaking hands, nodding, cordial. Then he came to the Boss. He froze Hague with a look, a curt "H'ya," and kept going. "Hague's face turned purple," Lepis wrote. "It was a political spanking, and its significance didn't escape anyone."

Harry Truman, cocky, a fighter, wasn't the kind of a man to forgive an affront like Hague's effort to dump him. When Truman pulled off the political upset of the century by defeating Thomas E. Dewey, Hague was dead as far as influence in Washington went, and his long rule quickly came to an end. In the city election of 1949, he was routed by an insurgent revolt headed by John V. Kenny, who had been one of his ward leaders. The result delighted Harry Truman, who remarked to Congressman Edward Hart, of Hudson County:

"Ed, I see the people of Jersey City finally got rid of that S.O.B. Hague."

Jersey City, however, had not freed itself of the incubus of the Hague machine. It had merely exchanged one boss for another. Kenny took over the Hague apparatus, and it continued to function much as it had in the past. The new boss never bestrode the state in the masterful manner of Hague; he made no "I am the law" boasts. But throughout the 1950s and 1960s he ruled the Hudson County Democratic machine; he was a power behind the throne in Democratic administrations in Trenton; his was the determining word in making key appointments. And public life in Jersey City was just as incredibly corrupt as it had been during the long rule of Hague.

Then, in 1969, the Nixon Administration did what Hague had feared Roosevelt might do in 1932. It sent a pair of tough federal prosecutors into New Jersey. Frederick B. Lacey, who had been a high-priced attorney representing many major corporate interests, was appointed U.S. Attorney, and he chose as his right-hand man and principal assistant a young, vigorous and determined prosecutor, Herbert J. Stern. Lacey and Stern opened an all-out war on official corruption, beginning by prosecuting the Newark city administration of Mayor Hugh J. Addonizio, a regime that had unsavory ties to Mafia leaders. After the conviction of Addonizio and his principal aides, Lacey was appointed to the federal district court, and Stern took over as U.S. Attorney.

Herbert Stern is short, dark-haired, sharp-featured. Physically he reminds one of consumer crusader Ralph Nader, and he has a Nader-like fervor and dedication when he investigates corruption. In 1970 he turned all this fire and energy against that long-time bastion of corruption—Hudson County and its reigning boss, John V. Kenny.

On November 16, 1970, after a months-long investigation, a federal grand jury spewed out a blizzard-like indictment. It contained thirty-four counts, and it charged that there had been one massive, on-going conspiracy over a period of years, during which the Kenny organization had extorted payoffs from every contractor doing business with the city and Hudson County. The cost, of course, had been borne by the taxpayers in the greatly inflated bills for everything from stationery to highway and bridge construction and the building of fire-houses.

Indicted were Boss Kenny himself; Mayor Thomas Whalen, of

Jersey City; Thomas Flaherty, President of the City Council; County Treasurer Joseph Stapleton; William J. Sternkopf, an influential member of the powerful Port of New York Authority; Hudson County Police Chief Fred J. Kropke; and others. Cynical New Jersey observers, recalling the half-century of Hague-Kenny immunity, were astounded that such charges had even been brought, and predicted that nothing would ever come of them.

For once, they were wrong. In one of the most sensational trials in New Jersey's history, Stern established through documentary records and the testimony of witnesses who had paid the bribes that it had been impossible to obtain city and county contracts without cash payoffs to the machine. The fee was usually 10 per cent of the contract price, and 10 per cent on hundreds of millions of dollars worth of public contracts over the years had resulted in huge, illicit fortunes.

One sequence in the months-long trial told the story. Stern showed from bank records that Mayor Whalen and Council President Flaherty had opened a joint, numbered, secret account in a Florida bank in November, 1968. Between this time and June 12, 1970—a period of only a little more than a year-and-a-half—the secret account swelled until it amounted to $1,231,438.50 in securities and cash. This enormous pile had been accumulated in such a short time, Stern emphasized, by a mayor who was making $30,000 a year and a city council president who was earning just $8,000.

The effect of this was devastating on a jury composed of ordinary citizens who had to struggle with such everyday problems as paying off the mortgage and meeting car payments. And so the jury did the incredible; it came in with a verdict—guilty as charged. Boss Kenny, whose case had been severed because he had had a heart attack, later pleaded guilty to six counts of income tax evasion.

Even more stunning than the convictions was the new precedent set in the sentencing of political bosses and officials in these New Jersey convictions. Federal judges established, for the first time in the nation, a consistent pattern of toughness in dealing with official corruption. In the past, political bosses and their official underlings, if they happened to be convicted, which in itself was a rarity, could almost count on slap-on-the-wrist penalties. The standard plea of a defense attorney went something like this: "Your Honor, my client has had a distinguished career. He has been a public official for decades; he has been honored, respected. [Here the attorney cites the fact that his client has, perhaps, taught Sunday School or headed a drive to help crippled kids. All his public honors are recited at great length.] Now he has been subjected to shame and humiliation; his family has suffered from his disgrace. Your Honor, I submit to you that this defendant has already been severely punished—more severely punished than by any sentence Your Honor might impose—and, therefore, I plead with Your Honor for a suspended sentence."

In the past, it had almost always worked. Convicted officials were fined; they were berated for their sins; and then they were given suspended sentences and permitted to retire to Florida, where they could sit on their money bags. Lincoln Steffens, who had a love for rogues and felt they shouldn't be jailed because the system had made them what they were, would doubtless have approved of such leniency. What has happened in the 1970s in the much-corrupted State of New Jersey assumes significance, therefore, because it represents such a complete break with the philosophy of the past.

Former Mayor Addonizio, of Newark, is serving a 10-year prison sentence. Mayor Whalen, of Jersey City, drew a 15-year term. Boss Kenny was sentenced to 18 years on his six guilty pleas, with the provision that this sentence might be revised, depending upon the report of federal prison doctors on the state of his health.

The philosophy behind such new stiff sentences holds the highly placed even more accountable, and more culpable, for their actions than the common man whose sins are usually minor compared to theirs. It was most eloquently expressed by Federal Judge George H. Barlow in sentencing Mayor Addonizio of Newark. The judge said:

"These were no ordinary criminal acts. These crimes were not the product of a moment of weakness, nor were they inspired by any of the defendant's desperate financial circumstances, nor were they the result of some emotional compulsion. These crimes for which Mr. Addonizio and the other defendants have been convicted represent a pattern of continuous, highly organized, systematic criminal extortion over a period of many years, claiming many victims and touching many more lives. . . .

"The criminal acts of these defendants were as calculated as they were brazen, as callous and contemptuous of the law as they were extensive. Nor can these defendants' criminal conduct be measured in dollars alone. It is impossible to estimate the impact upon—and the cost of—these criminal acts to the decent citizens of Newark, and, indeed, to the citizens of the State of New Jersey, in terms of their frustration, despair and disillusionment. How can we calculate the cynicism engendered in our citizens, including our youngsters, by these men? These very men—or some of them—who, as government officials, inveighed against crime in the streets, while they pursued their own criminal activities in the corridors of City Hall.

"Their crimes, in the judgment of this Court, tear at the very heart of our civilized form of government and of our society. The people will not tolerate such conduct at any level of our government, and those who use their public office to betray the public trust in this manner can expect from the courts only the gravest consequences." *

* The tough New Jersey attitude regarding offenses by high officials continues. In 1972 Secretary of State Paul Sherwin, long the close friend and right-hand man of Governor William T. Cahill, was indicted on charges of accepting a $10,000 campaign contribution from a road contractor who was seeking a highway contract. Shortly before this happened, Sherwin had bragged to newsmen in Trenton that the Jersey purge had involved mainly Democrats, and he had added that "the one thing I can promise you" was that Herbert Stern "will never get me." Stern, however, shortly afterwards broke the case against Sherwin, who was indicted by both federal and state grand juries. Tried in Freehold, New Jersey, in November, 1972, Sherwin was convicted, fined $2,000, and sentenced to one to two years in prison, a verdict that is now under appeal. The Secretary of State subsequently quit his $38,000-a-year post.

Dinner at Mark Hanna's home. Left, Mark Hanna;

right foreground, Ida and William McKinley.

Thanksgiving.
"For what we are about to receive, may the Lord make us truly thankful."

Cartoon from Puck.

Left, Theodore Roosevelt and Mark Hanna.

Mark Hanna.

Abraham Ruef.

Honorable Eugene E. Schmitz, Mayor of San Francisco.

Frank Hague.

John V. Kenny, mayor-elect of Jersey City, New Jersey.

7

———◆———

The Boss Still Lives

PROFESSORS IN THEIR ivory towers, newspaper columnists who sometimes write off the top of their heads, and various other pundits have predicted time and again that the political boss was about to become as extinct as the dinosaur. Events have always proved them wrong. It has not happened yet, nor is it likely to happen soon.

The demise of the political boss and his machine was forecast most frequently during the Roosevelt era of the 1930s. There was an element of surface logic behind the reasoning. It went like this: The base of power had shifted. Power was no longer in the hands of the political bosses in the big cities, but it was now concentrated in Washington. The billions of dollars being spent in new federal relief and work programs would undercut the local boss and his machine. They would no longer be the sole source of jobs and influence; the political structure in Washington would supersede them and eventually eliminate them.

This did not happen for fairly obvious, but almost universally overlooked, reasons. The enormous, new federal expenditures had to be handled on the local scene by local agents—in most instances, by those very political bosses and their machines whose extinction had been so prematurely predicted. The Hague machine was fairly typical of what happened in many areas across the nation. Its political influence was such that the vast federal expenditures, with all their attendant patronage, flowed through the hands of its designated agents. The Hague machine, of course, was Democratic, and the Democrats controlled Washington. Yet party labels did not really mean that much. In New Jersey, the rural counties were almost entirely dominated by Republican bosses and their machines, some of which have maintained their grip on their constituencies to this day; and it was astounding how these bosses, wheeling and dealing with their Democratic counterparts, managed to retain their influence and exercise a large degree of control over the New Deal largesse flowing out of Washington. The boss system in both parties flourished despite the new federal power complex that had been expected to doom it.

It is true, of course, that some political bosses have been dethroned and their machines splintered, but this has always happened periodically throughout our history. The Roosevelt expenditures, channeled largely through the independent LaGuardia administration in New York City, helped to reduce Tammany Hall from a tiger to a clawing kitten, but Tammany survived. It came back in full force in the postwar years under the leadership of Carmine DeSapio, who was finally exposed and sent to federal prison for playing a power-broker role in municipal corruption. In recent years, Tammany has been riddled with internal squabbles and suffered from the opposition activities of reform Democrats. But it would be entirely unrealistic to say that it is dead. Such ups-and-downs are typical of life, and there is nothing in the record to suggest that the down-era for a political machine is going to be permanent.

D. W. Brogan in his *Politics in America* makes the point that American urban society was "too incoherent, changing at too great speed and in too many ways, to provide a basis for an urban politics based on principles." He was writing in the early 1950s, but what was true then, and what was true of our historical past, is at least equally true today. The decades from 1950 to 1970 were marked by great internal migrations and shifting of population—Negroes moving from the South into the central cities of the North, Puerto Ricans and Mexican-Americans swelling urban and rural slums, workers changing jobs and residences in a highly mobile technological economy, urban dwellers fleeing to the suburbs; a population in a continuous state of flux. In such a chaotic society, there is little chance to put down deep roots; scant opportunity for the kind of co-ordinated, persistent effort that might result in Brogan's politics of principle. Yet, for the society to function at all, there has to be some apparatus, some means of managing the political structure. The management, the continuity that is essential, depends in most instances upon the political boss and his organization, the one fixed and stable medium of power.

Politics—the business of nourishing and managing a political machine—is a full-time job. It is a game played by professionals every weekday of the year and even on Sundays. The great bulk of the nation's citizens—preoccupied with family and jobs and the daily crises of life—simply cannot devote the attention to politics that politics demands; and so the manipulation of the political system falls, by default, into the hands of those whose major concern it is. There may be, as many argue, a "new politics," and to some extent there doubtless is, but the basic structures of American life and the American political organizations make it almost inevitable that political bosses will be with us for a long time to come.

What, then, can be expected for the future? Politics is never going to be a simon-pure endeavor. The dynamics of the political system require that the political boss must be able to reward his faithful followers; he must be able to find them jobs, to exercise influence where influence counts. The ground rules of the game make it virtually inevitable that our municipal, state, and federal bureaucracies will continue to have payrolls padded with more workers than are needed for the tasks to be performed. Just as certainly, influence will always be exercised in the awarding of contracts and the making of prestigious appointments. When all this has been acknowledged, however, there has to be a limit, a point of accountability, a recognition that there are standards even the most powerful boss must not transgress—and that a long prison term awaits him if he does.

Both Frederick Lacey, now a federal judge, and U.S. Attorney Stern in New Jersey have emphasized their belief that the colossal corruption of powerful political machines, unless it is stopped and punished, will tear American society apart. Both see the large-scale revolt of the younger generation as stemming in large part from the realization that the system at the top, in the interlocking power suites of politics and big business, has become so badly corrupted. Stern put it this way in one New York speech: "When they [the young] see men in high public office, men in responsible corporate positions, men with tremendous professional standing, violate the law while they . . . are told, by those very same men, that the law must be obeyed, they feel betrayed and they rebel against a system which they believe has played them false."

It is in this context that the New Jersey prosecutions of political bosses who went into partnership with the Mafia, who amassed multi-million-dollar fortunes through extortions and bribes, assume significance as setting a possible precedent for the future. Political bosses and their machines are facts of American life, but Americans do not have to tolerate a system that protects gangsters and lets corruption run wild. The heavy prison sentences imposed on officials in New Jersey say simply this: exposure of misdeeds is not enough; public humiliation is not enough. There must also be stiff punishment for "public officials who betray a public trust," for there is less excuse for a man in high position than there is for the slum dweller who, perhaps, is driven to crime by the hopelessness of his situation.

This is not a philosophy that is going to appeal to many at the top of our political structures, but it is the only one that can curb the vicious excesses of the political boss system and restore the faith of many Americans in their society and their government.

Bibliography of Sources

Bean, Walter. *Boss Reuf's San Francisco.* Berkeley: University of California Press, 1952.

Beer, Thomas. *Hanna.* New York: Alfred A. Knopf, 1929.

Brogan, D. W. *Politics in America.* New York: Harper Brothers, 1954.

Callow, Alexander B. *The Tweed Ring.* New York: Oxford University Press, 1966.

Flick, Alexander C. *Samuel J. Tilden.* New York: Dodd, Mead & Co., 1939.

Flynn, John T. *Men of Wealth.* New York: Simon & Schuster, 1941.

Josephson, Matthew. *The Politicos.* New York: Harcourt, Brace & Co., 1938.

Lynch, Denis Tilden. *"Boss" Tweed.* New York: Boni & Liveright, 1927.

McKean, Dayton David. *The Boss.* Boston: Houghton Mifflin Co., 1940.

Older, Fremont. *My Own Story.* New York: The Macmillan Co., 1926.

Steffens, Lincoln. *Autobiography of Lincoln Steffens.* New York: Harcourt, Brace & Co., 1931.

Stoddard, Lothrop. *Master of Manhattan, the Life of Richard Croker.* New York: Longmans, Green & Co., 1931.

Record of the Hudson trial in the U.S. Attorney's office, Newark, N.J.

Index

ABOUT THE AUTHOR

A journalist for twenty-five years and a free-lance writer since 1959, Fred Cook has had a varied career as a newsreporter, editor, re-write man, feature writer, and book author. Mr. Cook spent fifteen years with the *New York World-Telegram & Sun,* where his specialty was handling crime stories and crime-political inter-relationships. The recipient of many journalistic awards, he won the New York Newspaper Guild's Page One Award for best reporting or best magazine writing three times. It was in 1961 that Mr. Cook received the distinguished Sidney Hillman Award for "Gambling, Inc." in *The Nation.* Long interested in the social consciousness of America, he has written such well-received books as *The Warfare State, The FBI Nobody Knows,* and *The Corrupted Land.* In all, Mr. Cook is the author of some thirty-one books of nonfiction. A hard-working writer who frequently spends all seven days of the week at his desk meeting deadlines, Mr. Cook reports that sometimes, "when it all just gets to be too much," he plays hooky and goes fishing.

F79-188

320.973 Cook, Fred J.
COO
     American political
     bosses and
     machines

DATE			

F79-188